Cover photograph

ASDAR #036030
(*Naborr x Miss Dior)

Owners
Dr. Harvey A. Cohen
Melvin Powers

Visitors are welcome and Asdar can be seen at:

Champion Arabian Farm
24906 Jim Bridger Road
Hidden Hills, California 91302

THE ARABIAN HORSE

R. S. SUMMERHAYS

Foreword by Dr. Harvey A. Cohen

Cover photography by Polly Knoll

1976 EDITION

Published by
Melvin Powers
WILSHIRE BOOK COMPANY
12015 Sherman Road
No. Hollywood, California 91605
Telephone: (213) 875-1711

THE ARABIAN HORSE. © *R.S. Summerhays.*
First American edition published 1969 by
A. S. Barnes and Company, Inc., Cranbury,
New Jersey   08512

Library of Congress Catalogue Card Number: 74-83510

ISBN 0-87980-183-2
Printed in the United States of America

Printed by
HAL LEIGHTON PRINTING CO.
P.O. Box 1231
Beverly Hills, California 90213
Telephone: (213) 983-1105

Dedication

To my old friend and Founder of the Arab Horse Society
Henry Vyvyan Musgrave Clark
of Courthouse Arabian Stud
to whom I owe my introduction to
The Arabian Horse

Contents

Illustrations

ILLUSTRATIONS

FOREWORD

The purebred Arabian horse has been noted throughout history for his intelligence, beauty, strength, endurance, and a character that combines charm, gentleness, friendliness, and dignity with the fire of courage.

For thousands of years, the Arabian horse has been recognized as a distinct and valued breed. Tradition has it that Ishmael (son of Abraham) was the first man to mount a horse and that King Solomon presented to Arabs of the Azed tribe a magnificent stallion of the Ishmael line. From this stallion, the Azed tribe established the Zad-el-Rakeb line. The breed as we know it today traces back to that line.

In this book, R. S. Summerhays gives a readable and authoritative account of the Arab breed in the twentieth century, with primary emphasis on horses of Great Britain. *The Arabian Horse* should serve as a stimulating introduction for those who have not previously been acquainted with this noblest and most elegant of horses.

Few persons of our time have been more closely associated than has Mr. Summerhays with contemporary developments in the history of the Arabian horse, particularly in Great Britain. He became a member of the Council of the Arab Horse Society in 1920 and served as President of the Society from 1939 to 1946. At innumerable horse shows, he has judged all breeds and types of horses appearing in show rings in any capacity; and he has inspected and judged many hundreds of true Arabians. Himself an owner, he has ridden scores of noteworthy Arabians, as well as many other breeds. His knowledge of and his respect and affection for the Arabian horse are evident throughout his book.

During his long association with Arabians, Mr. Summerhays has been dedicated to the preservation of the purity and beauty of the breed. This dedication underlies all that he has written here; moreover, in Chapter Five, he spells out details of what he checks for when he inspects or judges Arabians. Some fifty photographs of notable Arabian horses illustrate the perfection of conformation and balance of the breed.

While British breeders have been in the forefront during the past hundred years in breeding and promoting the Arabian horse, there has been significant interest and enthusiasm in other European countries, particularly Poland. Mr. Summerhays devotes a chapter to discussion of the influence of Polish-bred horses that have been imported into England, especially since 1959. In his chapter on exports (from the British viewpoint, of course), he briefly analyzes the demand for Arabians in such countries as France, the Netherlands, Canada, and the United States. In the past, hundreds of English-bred Arabs have been brought into the United States, and there is ever-increasing interest in the breed here.

For more information about the breed, particularly in the United States and Canada, write to The International Arabian Horse Association, 224 East Olive Avenue, Burbank, California. If you are interested in registration of Arabian horses, write to The Arabian Horse Club Registry of America, 7801 Belleview Avenue, Englewood, Colorado.

Those of us here in the States who own and breed Arabians are delighted to share our enthusiasm and such knowledge as we have with others who want to learn more about the horse we consider the best and the most beautiful in the world. I have raised desert horses (Arabians), and I am enthralled by their proud gentleness, their spirit, and their beauty. If I can be of assistance to anyone who wants more information, please feel free to write or call me. Good luck.

Dr. Harvey A. Cohen

Champion Arabian Farm
24906 Jim Bridger Road
Hidden Hills, California 91302
Telephone (213) 888-1444

Introduction

I have no intention of referring more than lightly to the history of this most ancient of all breeds of horses, but only to tell of the Arabian horse as an inhabitant of these islands during the course of this century. References to earlier times and to the horse in other parts of the world will only be incidental to the main story. Let it be sufficient to mention the undisputed fact that every English Thoroughbred Racehorse is derived from three Arabian Horses, the Byerley Turk (imported in 1689), the Darley Arabian (1705) and the Godolphin Arabian (1728).

Many other Arabian sires occur in the pedigrees of our present day racehorses, but let this suffice. Were it necessary to make further the claims to fame for this breed, let me add that of the 100 and more distinct breeds and types of horses found throughout the world to-day the greater number have, throughout an immensity of time, either been founded on the Arabian horse or have had, for the sole purpose of improving or upgrading the particular breed or type, an infusion, more often than not repeated, of Arab blood.

The Arabian Horse can hardly complain of lack of publicity, for throughout the ages much has been written of his ancestry, his endurance and beauty, and fabulous prices were paid for this Asl (or Asil) horse, the word indicating a horse of noble lineage. It might be noted, too, that Kehilan (for we constantly come across the name when reading of the history of the horse) is the exact equivalent in meaning to our English word Thoroughbred. The Arabian is, as Lady Wentworth tells us, the Kehilan Ajuz, or Old

Thoroughbred, of the desert. It is claimed that the horse was known as far back as 5,000 B.C. and that enormous sums were paid for him for racing in Arabia, Egypt and Syria. It is claimed, too, that the breed was traditionally wild in Arabia and that the first wild horse to be captured was in Yemen by Baz, the great-great-grandson of Noah. This lovely breed of horses is very, very old, so old in fact that we cannot even place the approximate date of its origin, indeed, one might say it seems to have receded into the hands of the Gods.

What then of this horse in England to-day? Has he added to his stature, or is he losing ground to other breeds in the competition for usefulness and general desirability for pleasure and for sport? More important still, is he, as his detractors assert, just a toy, useless to the modern horseman, and is it correct to say, as someone wrote in the press recently; 'What is true about pet beagles applies with equal force to show Arabs?' Perhaps I can show how remote from the truth this is; how biased, and how steeped in prejudice. Is it to be assumed that because the beagle is brought to the family fireside and made a pet that he loses his hunting instincts? That may be true, but the theory is against the rules of heredity, and anyway, what applies to hound does not necessarily apply to horse.

In reviewing the literature of the Arabian Horse one recalls the names of great authorities, all of whom travelled the Arabian desert, some on several occasions, and shared the life of the Bedouins and their horses. Notable among these were Wilfrid Scawen Blunt and his wife, Lady Anne Blunt, grand-daughter of Lord Byron and mother of Lady Wentworth, the most important Arab breeder of more modern times and the breed's greatest publicist. Then we find such travellers, authorities and writers as Homer Davenport, with his notable, *My Quest of the Arabian Horse*, Spencer Borden, of *The Arab Horse* and Major R. D. Upton with his *Gleanings from the Desert of Arabia*, and Carl Raswan. Perhaps the most authoritative of all are the two books by Lady Anne Blunt, *The Bedouin Tribes of the Euphrates*, recording her impressions of her first journey, and her second book, *Pilgrimage to Nejd*.

There is no more fascinating history of the Arabian Horse than Lady Wentworth's *The Authentic Arabian Horse* and to a lesser extent, *The Thoroughbred Racehorse*. The details contained in these enormous books are almost without limit, and go into the ancestry and many other details of the horse from the age when records were made on stone.

Enough then of references to this horse most renowned through the centuries. My object in writing this book is to tell something of his progress since about the beginning of this present twentieth century. How did we find him then, how do we to-day? Have those who have nurtured him all these years been worthy of their trust, or have they failed in some way, however good their intentions may have been? At least this is a subject which should demand the greatest thought by all interested in the breed, whether breeder or owner. And surely of great importance, what of his future in this age when competition is at its most exacting?

R. S. S.

CHAPTER ONE

A Glimpse into the Past

Ever since the famous Byerley Turk, one of the three foundation sires of the English Thoroughbred, was imported into England, a considerable number of Arabian sires were brought to this country from time to time and used for breeding racehorses as well, no doubt, for the less illustrious saddle horse. Outside those few centres where racing was carried on, the Arab had made little visible impact in general upon the horse-world in England. He was, as he has been over the ages, used to improve a number of breeds in Great Britain and elsewhere, notable among these being the Hackney, that supreme representative of the harness horse, which breed roughly came into being at the time of the evolution of the English Thoroughbred. According to the best authority the Hackney breed derives from an Arab stallion named Blaze, who was by Flying Childers by the Darley Arabian out of a strong common bred mare, and the union produced the original Shales. That of course was many years ago.

No doubt largely because of its beauty and rather glamorous bearing, the Arab was later to become much in favour as a lady's hack, and one only has to look for proof of this at some of those delightful family paintings in our art galleries and stately homes. The ladies, in their flowing habits and charming hats, had chosen to ride Arab horses. How beautiful this combination was, and what a gracious addition to the equestrian scene.

During the last century riding for pleasure and recreation was mostly confined to the landed classes, the well-to-do professional and business men, and the larger tenant farmers. Hunting was the

14

chief form of equestrian sport and there is no doubt that a horse of greater substance and size was preferred, and presumed to have greater ability, than one showing the beauty and general elegance typified by the Arab. For the rest, and this must be looked at in the widest possible sense, those were the days of the harness horse, which, owing to the needs of commerce, the ever increasing size of the population and the long awaited improvement of the roads, was becoming more and more obvious and in demand.

Be all that as it may, many years were to pass before the Arab was to make even the smallest appeal to the general horse public in Great Britain. Long since had the racehorse owners and breeders, who after all were interested only in the horse which raced faster than its competitors, ceased to be interested in the Arab, which had created the very breed with which they were so vitally concerned. The demand for speed and more speed had largely changed the type and character of the Thoroughbred from that of the Arab from which it was descended. Nevertheless, throughout the world, and this fact will be emphasized from time to time, the Arab was imported by many countries to improve and generally upgrade the breed or breeds of the country concerned. Such importations were made not from England, as they are to-day, and have been throughout this present century, but mostly from Arabia itself. England had not then become the great exporter of the breed as it has been since the early twenties of this century.

In addition to this, and I speak of much more modern times, there were no horse-shows in the country providing classes solely for Arabs, and there were but very few studs producing them. The breed, except for Crabbet Park Stud, was really, for practical purposes, more or less non-existent in the country. Such few Arabs as there were to be found were mostly in the stables of re-tired Army officers and well-to-do individuals who recognised the breed's good qualities.

Before we go any further, let us consider the position of the few studs which existed in the days before the Arab Horse Society was founded in 1918—none of them, with the exception of the

Blunts' Crabbet Park, being of any size. As to this stud, I am indebted to Musgrave Clark for some details which cover the period 1897–1909. Not only are the numbers of stallions and mares recorded, but the colours also:—

Year	Stallions	Mares	Bay	Grey	Chestnut	Brown
1897	14	45	31	14	12	2
1898	17	44	30	13	15	3
1899	23	51	37	14	19	4
1900	29	50	39	14	23	3
1903	29	67	33	22	40	1
1908	33	43	30	12	29	5
1909	18	35	20	11	22	1

The greatest number of stallions and mares recorded was in the year 1903 when there were 96 in the stud. As this figure does not include colts, fillies or foals, the number of pure-bred Arabians at any one time must have been very impressive indeed, perhaps three or four times as many as are to be found to-day at any stud. Taking the top figures, what a picture is presented of stables housing 33 stallions or having 67 mares about the place! If we take the lowest figures, I fancy nowadays a stud owner would feel he had enough on his plate with 14 stallions and 35 mares.

In those days this famous stud held bi-annual sales, and of these Musgrave Clark writes; 'The late George Ruxton and I attended these sales, and one could buy a very nice mare for 100 guineas'. The many who to-day are more than anxious to buy 'a very nice mare' will read this with envy in their hearts. I am afraid they would not be able to buy even a not very nice mare for under three or four times that amount.

The traditional colour of the desert Arabian was bay, and it will be noticed that this quite lovely colour predominated. A little surprising is the fact that grey, which I fancy the not too well-informed believe to be the traditional colour for the Arab, is a bad third to chestnut, now by far the colour most in evidence. Brown is in poor supply in any breed, including the Arab.

Enough at the moment of the Blunt Arabs. Of the other studs

Naseel. Grey Stallion
(Raftan/Naxina). (Photo
by Miles Bros.)

Naseel. Grey Stallion
(Raftan/Naxina).

Benjamin. Bay Stallion (Champurrado/Baranova). (Photo by Photonews)

Bahram. Chestnut Stallion (Sanfoin/Betina). (Photo by Miles Bros.)

to be found in the country in pre-Society days there is little to be said. A familiar figure at the Society's Annual Show has, up to very recently, been that of the late Miss M. C. E. Lyon who had a stud not only in England, but in Ireland also; this I believe she inherited, and she certainly claimed it as one of the oldest and biggest, when both were considered as one.

I am not sure which was the oldest, but Miss Ethelred Dillon of Charlbury, Major Roger Upton of the 7th Lancers and the Rev. Furze Vidal of Needham Market all had studs, and all were noted enthusiasts in their day. There was, too, the Hon. George Savile, whose stud at Thames Ditton was well known. Musgrave Clark, of course, and George Ruxton were among those who laid the very foundations upon which the Arab Horse Society of to-day was built.

With so few Arabs in the country then, and with a negligible interest in the breed, it is not surprising that there were no shows to cater for the Arab. On this subject it is interesting to read what A. A. Dent, that great delver into the histories of so many breeds of horses, has to say. Just over one hundred years ago, he tells us, was held possibly the first class in which Arabs were shown, but even then they were combined with other breeds. A class was held at the Agricultural Hall, London, for 'Eastern-bred horses' in 1864, and he writes that the class attracted three Barbs and six Arabs, the prize money of £20 being divided between the best Barb and the best Arab. Apparently the class was looked upon as something of a failure, for in the following year it was cancelled. There were similar classes for Eastern horses held from time to time at the Hurlingham Polo Club in London, but they seemed to have had but little support, even among the polo players, for which game the Arab, in those days, was considerably in demand.

As some indication of the lack of interest in the Arab in the early days of the century I give some details of the number of entries of Arab *and Barb* stallions, not exceeding 14·2 h.h., which were shown at the Agricultural Hall, Islington, London, at that time. Some of these were Officers' Chargers brought home from

India, Egypt and Malta, and the Show was held under the auspices of the National Pony Society, which had been formed in 1893. What is particularly interesting about these classes is that they were stallion classes, especially introducing the entrants as polo pony sires. How different from these days when the stallion is shown as a sire for producing Anglo-Arabs or part-bred Arabs to be used as riding horses and ponies, or for upgrading and as an accepted infusion of blood for any type or breed of light horse. Here are the entries at the Agricultural Hall:—

6 — 1900	7 — 1906
9 — 1901	8 — 1908
8 — 1903	9 — 1909
4 — 1905	7 — 1910

As the Arabs shared these with the Barbs it is hardly an impressive list.

The period which I intend this book to cover is roughly that since the beginning of this century, an almost negligible period in terms of Arabian horse history, which goes back for so very many centuries. The Arab in this latter half of the 20th century is, with the exception of the racehorse, whose value is based entirely on its ability to race or jump faster and better than its opponents, probably the most saleable of all breeds of horses in the British Isles to-day, commanding better average prices and being acceptable in more parts of the world than any other breed save, as I say, the Thoroughbred. Does this not give cause for some wonderment? The Arab Horse Society was founded in 1918 and held its first show, appropriately, in view of the association with the racehorse, at Newmarket on 4th March, 1919, a second being held three months later at Ranelagh Club in London. In the following year the first Arab show was held at the Agricultural Hall at Islington in London, which for many years was its established home. The entries at all these early shows were understandably small, but in 1966, 48 years after the foundation of the Society, the entry was 252, excluding Anglo-Arabs and Part-bred Arabs.

What circumstances were responsible for this rise in the popularity of the breed?

That a number of factors led to this happy state of affairs is certain, but to say that it is due primarily to the beauty of the breed and its inherent qualities of intelligence and soundness, however near that may be to the truth, does not present an exact picture. We must remember that since the second world war, the very period during which the Arab's popularity became more and more noticeable, all breeds, with the exception of the harness horse, showed an increase in numbers and a larger measure of public interest. Interest in the horse had been awakened, and a new riding public had appeared. Interest has been particularly keen in the case of our Mountain and Moorland breeds, especially the Welsh Mountain and New Forest ponies.

The true cause and the satisfactory results are not hard to find, but we must go back to a time somewhere towards the end of the second decade of the century for them. No doubt when we look at the march of events in the horse world and consider the number of breed societies now existing, the Arab Horse community would have sooner or later formed a Society to look after its interests. Nonetheless, all credit must be given to the two enthusiasts who conceived the idea and, in fact, launched the Arab Horse Society in 1918, in spite of the fact that there were only a handful of breeders and no more than perhaps 120 mares in the country, of which about one half were in the possession of one stud—Crabbet Park, Sussex.

In that year two enthusiastic horsemen were enjoying one of their frequent lunches at the Albion Hotel, Brighton, Sussex. They were H. V. Musgrave Clark, a breeder of Arabs for nearly 70 years, and the Rev. D. B. Montefiore, who, between them, formed the idea of a Society to foster the breeding and importation of pure-bred Arabs, and to encourage the re-introduction of Arab blood into English light-horse breeding. Montefiore was a well-known breeder of polo ponies and was well aware of the suitability of the Arab for the game. In 1903 he had been elected

President of the National Pony Society, the guardians of the polo pony and our Mountain and Moorland breeds. In 1918 then, the Arab Horse Society was formed with Montefiore as Secretary and Wilfrid Scawen Blunt, the father of Lady Wentworth, as President. Clark was already an experienced breeder of Arabs, having started his stud at Eltham in Kent in 1900 with four pure Arab mares. I was elected to the Council two years later.

Some idea of how it has fared, and of more importance, how the breed has fared under the guidance of its Council, I will endeavour to show in the following chapters. It must be remembered, however, that this was a period when most breeds in the country were, paradoxically, showing inflationary tendencies, for their growth coincided with the virtual elimination of the harness horse for commerce and pleasure. The horse for riding had taken the place almost entirely of the harness horse.

It is well to note, before going any further, the definitions of the Pure-bred Arab, the Anglo-Arab and the Part-bred Arab, as required by the Stud Books issued by the Society as, of course, without such entry, no horse can be shown at the Society's Shows. This qualification applies to most of the shows (of which at the moment there are over 50) which offer classes for them. The definitions are:

Arabian horses are those in whose pedigree there is no other than Pure Arabian blood.

Anglo-Arabs

1. Horses in whose pedigree there is no strain of blood other than Thoroughbred or Arab. To comply with this condition Thoroughbreds must be entered, or eligible for entry, in the G.S.B. and Arabs entered, or eligible for entry, in the G.S.B. (Arab Section) or the Arab Horse Stud Book.

2. Anglo-Arabs bred in foreign countries entered, or eligible for entry, in the recognised Stud Books of those countries may also be accepted for registration if approved by the Council.

Part-bred Arabs. Arabs for entry in the Part-bred Arab Register are limited to those animals who have either one great-grand parent of pure Arab blood or two great-grand parents of pure Arab blood.

At the same time one might consider the requirements of the now well established Brood Mare Premium Scheme, although, in fact, this was instituted at a much later date. This is designed to encourage the use of the Arab in breeding horses of Arabian type, and consists of the offering of super and other premiums by the Society, assembled annually at given centres, to such mares of various breeds (divided into large and small types) as the judges may decide. To qualify for entry all mares must produce a certificate that they have been served by an Arab or Anglo- (but not part-bred) Arab, or that they have produced a living foal.

It may be of some interest to note the constitution of the first Council. It will be noticed that the President was Wilfrid Scawen Blunt. Musgrave Clark tells us that this office would have been held by Blunt's wife, Lady Anne, but she had died at their Stud at Cairo in 1917. In fact, he says, Scawen Blunt was never aware that he had been appointed to this office and he died shortly after the formation of the Society.

PATRON   Prince Feisal of Arabia
PRESIDENT   Wilfrid Scawen Blunt
VICE-PRESIDENT   Sydney G. Hough

COUNCIL

Captain E. G. Atkinson	Colonel W. A. MacDougall
Walter Lloyd Beale	Lord Middleton
Everard Calthrop	Major G. B. Ollivant
H. V. Musgrave Clark	A. M. Pilliner
A. Cochrane	George Ruxton
Captain L. Edmunds	Captain the Hon. George Savile
C. W. Laird	Colonel P. D. Stewart
Captain J. Hamilton Leigh	Colonel J. Hanson Tapp
D. P. MacDougall	R. A. Willis

SECRETARY
Rev. D. B. Montefiore

CHAPTER TWO

Progress

In the 48 years of its existence the Arab Horse Society has had only three Secretaries; I have not counted the fourth for he has only been in office a short while. It has been lucky in having so few, lucky in having men of character and understanding most suitable to their office and, even more so, in their dedication to the welfare of the breed whose future in the country has been so very much in their hands.

In 1936 Montefiore resigned after a long spell of 18 years; by that time he had become a sick man and for a considerable period had conducted much of the Society's work from his bed. Over the years I got to know him very well, and in my opinion his knowledge of the polo pony, and indeed all the other breeds of ponies which came under the umbrella of the National Pony Society, was of great indirect value to the Arab Society. In those days the Arab was used for polo and, had not the height limit for the polo pony been removed, thus introducing the small Thoroughbreds, and part Thoroughbred ponies, the Arab would be in far greater use for this purpose to-day.

There is perhaps some question about this, however, for I remember the late Colonel C. D. Miller who learnt the game with his two brothers in India, and who had much to do with its introduction and growth in popularity here, telling me that, in his experience, the Arab had too much sense to face up to the rough riding-off required by the game. Colonel Miller will be remembered by many of the older members of the Arab Society as Manager of the Roehampton Polo Club, where the Society held its show for many happy years. Although not essential, I believe that it is a good thing for a breed society's secretary to be a horseman, or at least to have been concerned in some way or another with the horse world. There is a lot in being able to speak the language of the horse.

Following the resignation of 'Monty', the Society found in his successor a real champion of the Arab in Brigadier W. H. Anderson, C.B.E., a retired Indian Cavalry Officer who gave 15 years of distinguished service to the breed. Anderson had a great knowledge of horses and was associated with his brother, General Anderson, in the running of their Thoroughbred stud at Newmarket. Among other activities, the former was the official referee at Roehampton Polo Club and had his own stud of Arabs at Newmarket. Because of these many connections with the horse world, and with his knowledge of the Arab in the East, he was very largely responsible for introducing and encouraging horsemen in England to breed the Arab.

It must never be forgotten that at that time, and for many years before, the Arab, by reason probably of it having but few horsemen to champion it, was not only out of favour, but often loudly and contemptuously decried. In any event, few even had the opportunity to see an Arabian horse. It was too small for the hunting-man, said the critics, it was just a pretty plaything of no use for the horseman and, in any case, out of favour so far as the polo player was concerned. Why bother with it? Of what use was it? This was clearly a case of finding the man at the right moment to fit the job.

In 'Willie' Anderson the Society found not only a champion of the breed, but a man who inspired great confidence and respect. He introduced to the Council a number of retired Army Officers who had served in the East, whose ability and understanding of the breed he vouched for, and progress was recorded in all directions, most marked being the increase in membership and the number of studs appearing all over the country. To the regret of all, Anderson fell gravely ill and never recovered, indeed he lingered for a long period, a great sufferer. It is doubtful whether the Society will ever find anyone, whether Secretary or otherwise, who will do so much as he did, for he came on the Arab scene when one was almost ashamed to say one bred or owned an Arab horse. Willie Anderson had charm, humour and a way of endearing himself to all.

We then come to the period as Secretary of Robert Askin (Colonel R. C. de V. Askin, M.B.E., M.C.), another retired regular Army Officer who knew the Arab in the East. Taking over in 1951 he found a very different state of affairs from that which had confronted Anderson when he assumed the Secretaryship. Here was a well established Society with a considerable membership; little did he realize that, almost from that very time, the Arab Horse Society was about to grow in a way which surprised us all. Little did any of us realise, for instance, that largely because of the influence of one horse, Mrs S. A. Nicholson's famous grey stallion, Naseel, the pony world would become hugely interested in the Arab as a sire for part-bred show ponies, and would rival the Thoroughbred for this purpose. Naseel's progeny have received very many awards at the major shows in England and at lesser shows even more. Irrespective of the show pony, the number of Arabs in the country was constantly increasing, new small studs were appearing and the Anglo-Arab (the Arab crossed with a Thoroughbred) was firmly established, even if only in a small way.

In consequence, the increase in membership of the Society and, of course, the registration of an ever-growing number of Arabs, Anglo and part-bred Arabs showed interest in the Arab to be booming. Beyond all this, Askin was to face an even bigger Arab Horse Show; what had once been a pleasant and comfortable job for a retired officer was now more than a full-time affair. As I know all too well, the Society of the early twenties was a very different kettle of fish from that served up to Arab lovers of 1965.

Quite unperturbed, Robert Askin carried on giving great service to a Society which had, during his term of office, become recognised as perhaps (excepting of course the Thoroughbred) England's most important breed society. I would like to conclude this reference to a most able Secretary by saying that he, unlike his predecessors, retired from office in 1965 in the best of health with surely the satisfaction of knowing that he left the Society too in the same state. The breed, whose well-being was so much in his hands, numbered in the country at least 100 stallions while the mares numbered many hundreds, with colts and fillies in large numbers. Save for the United States of America there is no country in the world where so many Arabs are to be found. How very many of us hold Colonel Askin in gratitude and in affectionate regard!

Before I pass to other matters it is interesting to note that in 1964 no fewer than 54 important shows in the country gave classes for Arabs, Anglo-Arabs and part-bred Arabs. Time was when, in order to encourage the showing of Arabs, the Council subsidised certain shows by way of prize money and/or rosettes. Such a course has long since been abandoned as being quite unnecessary, the various Shows finding little difficulty in filling the classes and providing the necessary prize money. This was one of the sure ways of introducing the breed to the show-going public thus ensuring its popularity.

To-day the main work of the Secretary, apart from the organisation of the Annual Show, is compiling, entering the almost daily additions and issuing, from time to time, three Stud Books; the Arabian, Anglo-Arab and Part-bred Arab. The Society, even in its early days, issued a periodical journal or magazine and does so to-day under the title of *The Arab Horse News*. The work of the Editor fell upon Anderson and, later, Askin. Fortunately for the latter this important job was taken over by Miss Margaret Greely, who carries it out most devotedly and with marked success. It is fortunate that in this Editor the Society has one who has been for many years a successful breeder of Arabs in a small way, and who undoubtedly has an exceptional 'eye' for the breed.

The Society has been very fortunate in its Patrons too, and as I write this we have Her Royal Highness Princess Alice, Countess of Athlone occupying this position. As our Patron, Princess Alice, who for a number of years has shown quite exceptional interest in the Society, has been a regular visitor to the annual show, arriving early and staying late. Her knowledge of the breed impresses and her charm delights us all.

Of the Presidents little need be said, except that it is no mere ornamental office, because whoever is honoured by such an appointment must anticipate a busy time, for apart from being in constant, almost day to day touch with the Secretary, he presides at all Council Meetings and many others. Looking down the long list of past Presidents, as I have said, Wilfrid Scawen Blunt was the first, and he was followed by the late Sidney G. Hough, who held office for one year; his son, Cecil Hough, became President ten years later. A wise and sound Councillor he has served four terms as President. Furthermore, Cecil Hough has exhibited at every one of the Society's shows since 1923 (42 consecutive shows). A remarkable and, I think, unique effort. I occupied the same office for 7 years, but I should add that these years covered the period of the Second World War when, to a large extent, everything was in abeyance. I was, in fact, a night watchman for the Arab horse. It is interesting perhaps to note that I was followed by two of the greatest breeders of Arabians of our time (Musgrave Clark having consistently refused to hold this office), the late Lady Wentworth, and in the following year, the late Miss G. M. Yule.

Now we come to 1965 and the retirement of Colonel Askin. Three Secretaries in 47 years, and the appointment of Lt.-Colonel J. A. Crankshaw, M.C., to the post. How did he find the state of the Society? A glance at the figures for certain previous years is illuminating. First to deal with registrations:

	1965	1964	1963	1951
ARABS	210	221	180	91
ANGLO-ARABS	49	50	40	11
PART-BREDS	682	679	508	127
	951	950	728	229

In addition to the recording and issuing certificates in respect of 951 animals, it is surprising to note that, in the course of a year, there were issued 638 transfers of ownership. Exports were made to eleven countries.

There were more than 1200 members of the Society at the end of 1965.

In 1966 entries for the Annual Show exceeded 600 (603 in fact), while the not unsubstantial figure of £500 was paid in the form of premiums under the Brood Mare Premium Scheme.

Finally, the Winston Churchill Cup presented annually since 1947 at the Royal International Horse Show, when the winners of every riding breed (pony classes excluded) taking part in the Show compete, the winner being judged by the volume of public applause. In the 19 years of this competition the Arab has gained the cup six times.

CHAPTER THREE

The Annual Show

For various reasons the Society has had to change the site of its annual Show on several occasions. I have already referred to the early shows held at the Agricultural Hall, Islington, London. This venue was the scene of quite a horse show festival, for various Societies held their shows there—the Hunters (The Hunters Improvement and Light Horse Breeding Society), the Ponies (The National Pony Society), jointly with the Arabs, the Shires (Shire Horse Society) and at a very early date the Hackneys (Hackney Horse Society). The month of March does not see London at its best and Islington was then a far from attractive district. Yet these annual gatherings of so many of the country's finest horses and ponies brought to 'The Hall' (as it was often called) large numbers of seriously minded horsemen, for these were really breed shows designed to draw breeders and others from all parts of the country and from abroad, which they certainly did. In spite of the surroundings all these shows were very popular, and it is worth recording that the polo pony was the most important feature at the Pony Show. After the second world war 'The Hall' was no longer available and became just a memory, to many of us a very happy one.

The next move for the Arab Show (and this was in effect turning the indoor spring show into an open air summer one) was to the Roehampton Polo Club with a setting about as different from Islington as could well be imagined, for Roehampton was, and is, a charming place, having a large number of loose boxes about as conveniently handy as could be. At about the same time the

International Horse Show left the arched-roof of Olympia and went into the open—to the (sometimes) blue skies of the White City.

The Society's stay at Roehampton was much enjoyed by all, and was probably one of the most elegant shows to be held in the country, but after a few years, when polo ceased to be played there, the Club became largely a social, golf, lawn-tennis and croquet affair. In fact, for the two days of the Show one of the golf holes had to be given over to the Arab, not I think (and naturally enough) very willingly, by some of the golfers. Here we had the advantage of unlimited stabling, anyway more than enough for our purposes; and not only this, the stables were close to the show ring and, looking across the show ground to the tree-surrounded golf course away to Richmond Park, we had a show in peaceful and really lovely surroundings. In addition the Club extended the facilities of their restaurant for the entertainment of our Patron, President and other V.I.Ps. It was all very pleasant and I am sure that, when the time came for us to leave, one and all were desperately sorry. The golfers had won the day. Polo had been ousted from the grounds, and the last was seen of the horse when the Arabs moved on.

The Society's next show-ground was the one which is used now, and had been used for many years, by the Richmond Royal Horse Show, but we were there for one year only, 1958. In these surroundings of a different character it was natural enough that comparisons were inevitably made with the immediate past, and they were not very encouraging. I think few were disappointed when negotiations for holding the show there in the following year came to nothing. So we moved on again and this time to a racecourse.

To move to such a setting was not entirely new to the horse world for I seem to remember judging years previously at Derby Racecourse, and the Hackney Horse Society had been there too, I think, while the now famous Ponies of Britain Club had, as the result of the enthusiasm and foresight of Mrs Glenda Spooner,

29

staged their show at Royal Ascot Racecourse. It was she who told me that, during the course of her negotiations for a show ground, she had been in touch with the Kempton Park Racecourse Authority and strongly urged me to approach them. This I did, of course, through the Committee of the Arab Horse Society who lost no time with the negotiations and in 1959 the Show staged its first appearance there. A happy occasion indeed.

Again, of course, there were the inevitable criticisms; mostly these were concerned with the considerable distance, although within the confines of the ground, of the great range of boxes used by the racehorses. Although many of these are always used, the criticism has been largely met by the erection annually of a large number of temporary boxes within a very short distance of the show arena. I think it is correct to say that to-day all are very well satisfied with the move to Kempton Park. The surroundings are delightful, although the railway is separated from the show ground only by a thick belt of trees. Trains (but not too many of them) can certainly be heard and seen, and while a few of the horses show some surprise at this it appears of very small moment. Thanks to the courtesies shown by the Racecourse Committee and the facilities and terms offered, we have reason to be very satisfied and grateful. Here we are then at Kempton and long may we remain there.

So long as I can remember complaints have been made about the poor attendances at the Arab Society's Shows, and these were heard even in the old Islington days. Many suggestions have been made, and many of them carried out, with a view to the show making a more popular appeal. Jumping and driving classes, classes for riders and drivers in costumes and so on, but none of these apparently made much difference to the attendances. Adverse comparisons were made with the attendances at the Hunter's Improvement and Light Horse Society and the Ponies of Britain Shows, both of which, it is true, draw far bigger gates, but these were not, nor are they now, fair comparisons.

Take the Hunter Show, or rather shows, for there are the Spring and Summer Shows. The number of people who are actively interested in the hunter is far greater than those who 'follow' the Arab for, apart from the hunters, the Stallion Show is a show mainly of the Thoroughbred, which is, first and foremost, the horse which sires not only most of the hunters, but many of the country's riding horses too. Again at the Spring Hunter Show one can see the horse which is, or is to become, one's local stallion which sires the majority of hunters and hacks in the neighbourhood.

And take too the case of the Ponies of Britain Shows—the Annual Stallion Show and the two summer shows. Apart from the most loyal support given by its members to these most splendidly run shows, they cater not for three breeds only, as does the Arab Show (pure bred, Anglo-Arab and Part-bred Arab), but for nine Mountain and Moorland as well as a number of other classes under various categories. Every one of these native pony societies are to-day enjoying various degrees of popularity, having very satisfactory memberships and showing increasing export returns. Particularly does this apply to the Welsh Mountain Pony and the New Forest, both of which enjoy large memberships. Pony breeding, pony showing and pony ownership have never been embraced by so many people with so much enthusiasm.

Under the circumstances it has become generally recognised that to look for large attendances at the Arab Show is unreasonable, but to anticipate a steady increase is something to be striven for, and this desirable state of affairs appears to be established, as for several years past the number of those who attend shows a steady increase.

My own more active association with the horse world, covering at least half a century, leads me to the conclusion that it is really divided into groups specialising in particular breeds or activities, and that those who are interested in the horse, *whatever the breed and wherever it is found*, are comparatively few. By this I mean people who can recognise a breed at sight, who know the requirements for its conformation, something of its history, for what work it is most suited and so on. To have this knowledge, even to a modest degree, is a great privilege, and to have judged, as I have, all breeds and types of horses appearing in the show rings to-day in any capacity, including harness classes, is, of course, a rare privilege.

For this reason I would like to see more of the horse world visiting the Arab Show, not only because the more breeds one looks at with an eye intent on acquiring knowledge of the sort particularly applicable to the breed the better, but because they would see at the Arab Show, first and foremost, a breed which is surely the one which displays the most refined, the most elegant and, as few will dispute, the world's most beautiful horse? More people would thus be won over to the breed, for the Society is lucky in having something very special to offer. I have felt that one way this could be done would be by sending a number of complimentary show tickets each year to the more prominent members of other breed societies and to prominent persons in the horse-world. Nothing would be lost, new breeders and owners and members would be gained and, in any event, it is more than probable there would be just those many more who would praise the Arabian Horse.

As I write this it is nearly 50 years since the Arab Society was formed. That this horse has gained enormously in popularity and in various other ways is certain and remarkable.

Whether the Arab has improved or deteriorated as a breed is a matter which I will deal with later. It may be there are a few who would not wish to see the membership of the Society grow, nor the show expand in entries and attendances. It is true that those of us who have known the Show for, say, at least a couple of decades, have had really immense enjoyment from the annual gatherings round the ropes, where old friends have been met again, present-day affairs discussed and, of course, more than anything, the entries criticised. I feel, and I know this is shared by many, that the annual Arab Show is the most family affair of any, for it seems to have a combination of more elegance, graciousness and friendli-

Zehros. Bay Stallion (Argos/Zehraa).

Obadiah. Grey Stallion (Iridos/Trypolitanka).

Burkan. Grey Stallion (Saladin II/Biruta).

Blue Halo. Chestnut Stallion (Blue Domino/Aleya).

Princess Amara. Chestnut Mare (Greatheart/-Princess Troubadour). (Photo by J. Weston)

Darjeel. Chestnut Stallion (Dargee/Rajjela).

Autumn Sunshine. Grey Mare (Blue Magic/Trypolitanka). (Photo by Photonews)

Autumn Velvet. Bay Mare (Blue Magic/Trypolitanka).

ness than any other show. Perhaps, however, this may be our imagination or prejudice, or both, born of our admiration for the breed, but I think this is not entirely so. I have served on the Councils or Committees of most of the breed and other Societies, and over many years attended an exceptional number of shows, large and small, and yet, reviewing this fact and recalling so many happy times, I always come back to the feeling that the show most looked forward to, and the one most enjoyed by me, is the Arab.

It would never do for the breed to stand still and this applies to all others too, for to do so inevitably means that popularity tends to wane and with that comes inevitable depreciation. The Show is the shop-window for all breeds and the Arab is no exception, for it is vital to preserve the conformation and type of every breed. This is more than ever necessary in the case of the Arab, which, after all, in appearance has more outstandingly notable features than any other breed, not excepting the mighty Shire horse. What breed has a more arresting head, croup, tail carriage, a more typical action, and what more unforgettable than the whole bearing and carriage of the high-class Arabian stallion?

It is not everyone, especially in these days, who can afford the time and money to visit the many studs now to be found in all parts of the country. Enjoyable and instructive as it undoubtedly is to see as many as one can, even so there is nothing to touch the annual show. For this reason alone it is necessary for the show to increase in reputation, for its judges to be of the highest qualifications and of the greatest integrity. As the years go by the number of visitors from abroad increases, and they come to the show to see the best. This has been looked upon as so important that each year a host or hostess is appointed, not only to answer any enquiries, but to see that these visitors feel they are welcome and meet members most likely to be of help; an excellent idea of course.

The show is held on two consecutive days, the first being devoted to the Pure-bred, the second to the Anglo-Arab and Part-bred. As far as I can remember it has always been held in this way, and as it is found that, generally speaking, the programme can be carried out punctually without undue stress or strain, so it is likely to remain. Certainly, the Society cannot be accused of not making good use of their shop window!

The Ponies of Britain Club hold their Shows at Ascot, Kelso and Peterborough and the National Pony Society have adopted the practice of moving to various, widely separated parts of the country. These policies seem to have met with success and I think no one could say truly that the latter have been unwise in not remaining year after year at the same show ground where, by the way, they often shared the week with the Arabs. In these days of ever-increasing costs in every respect, and transport in particular, many exhibitors away in the country are gravely concerned at the cost of transport every year. At least it can be said, in the case of the above shows, they are doing something to overcome a real trouble. It is found, too, that by going into the provinces the various people concerned locally are stimulated, resulting in a widening interest and increased financial advantages to the Show.

Against this must be considered the fact that the particular show ground gains a kind of proprietory value for a show, and just as in the old days one referred to The Hall and Roehampton, so to-day we refer to a horse winning at Kempton. Obviously the question to be answered is whether the Arab Show would gain in the number of entries or increase its takings, or both, if it moved each year to different parts of the country. This is debatable, but in view of the steady increase under both these headings, the answer would appear to be fairly emphatically in the negative. The day may come when the Society will find it necessary to hold perhaps a second annual show in the north. This could be a good thing, but not yet I fancy. The advantages to-day of being at Kempton are great. The show ground is delightful, the facilities are very considerable and we are with friends.

CHAPTER FOUR

Some Unusual Publicity

The Second World War broke out during my first year as President of the Society, and as most of the breed societies became dormant during the duration of the war I remained in office throughout that period. Most of the established shows suspended all activities but, nonetheless, a surprisingly large number of small shows were staged up and down the country, mostly in aid of the Red Cross or War charities of various descriptions. Hitherto, except for the Society's own show, the International, the Royal, Richmond and Bath and West, the Arab in the show ring was largely unknown. Taking advantage of this state of affairs we were able to introduce the Arab to the provinces and to various somewhat remote parts of the country, which was obviously a good thing for the breed.

This was, however, something of a mixed blessing, for various bad Arabians walked away with top prizes owing to lack of competition and often, I am afraid, through lack of competent judges. This was natural enough, for judges had to be found and these, often through nobody's fault, were with little or no knowledge of the breed. Thus many owners found themselves owning a horse upon which a false value had been placed, while others had their good exhibits denigrated.

Remaining as President all through the war and, in fact, until 1946, I was able to arrange, immediately after the war, and entirely through the whole-hearted co-operation of the Show Committee and, of course, breeders, what proved to be a wonderful display of Arab stallions at the Royal Windsor Show. There were no awards and indeed no placings. Labour was very short and with petrol restrictions transport was extremely difficult, yet in spite of all this twenty-three stallions were shown in hand and occupied the ring for fifteen minutes while I gave a running commentary over the public address system. It was beyond question the best and biggest parade of pure Arab stallions ever seen in the country up to that time. That the owners of all these lovely horses should have gone to the great trouble and expense of sending them, many from long distances, without hope of reward, financial or otherwise, was the clearest evidence of the affection, pride and enthusiasm in which the breed was held.

Also during my term of office another and even greater display of Arabs was seen, this time at our first show at Roehampton Club. At that show, so very different from the spacious ring at Windsor, we had the Championship class for Stallions and no fewer than twenty-nine stallions were shown in the very small ring. This, in fact, was on the disused hard tennis courts which now I think are part of, or immediately adjoining, the Rosslyn Park Rugby Football Ground. A class of so many stallions was of course unique. Whether such a number has been exceeded in the States, where the Arab flourishes to-day in great numbers, I cannot say, but we had never seen anything like it here, and I doubt if we ever shall again.

It was for the judges, Brigadier R. S. Scott and myself, an extremely anxious time. There were twenty-nine stallions in a ring only big enough to take say fifteen or so at the outside, and for safety we had to eliminate many of those presumed to be among the 'also-rans'. It was, by the way, in another class at this show, that we found a miserable looking little yearling colt, much smaller than all the others and in the poorest condition, obviously suffering from worm trouble, which we placed first. He was in fact Dargee, later bought by Lady Wentworth, and was to become famous on both sides of the Atlantic. Dargee probably won more championships and first prizes than any other Arab stallion in my time.

Silver Grey. Grey Mare (Royal Diamond/Silver Gilt). (Photo by John Nestle)

Silver Sheen. Grey Mare (Bright Shadow/Silver Grey). (Photo by John Nestle)

Hassani of Fairfield. Bay Stallion (Rissani/Hadassa). (Photo by Photonews)

Iridos. Grey Stallion (Irex/Rafeena). (Photo by John Nestle)

If these two occasions of Arabians in bulk were a wonderful advertisement for the breed, another outstanding piece of publicity was given repeatedly, and in many parts of the country, by the late Henry Wynmalen on his lovely grey Shagya-Arabian, Basa. Later Basa's place was taken by Basca, a part-bred Arabian standing 17·1 h.h. These were memorable displays of dressage and made even more interesting by the running commentary given by his wife, Julia. One can only hope that time will produce other such beautiful horses ridden by other accomplished riders. As recently as the Society's Show in 1964 an extremely beautiful and talented display was given by Miss Jennie Bullen (now Mrs Loriston-Clarke) on the Champion Show Hack, the black mare, Desert Storm, by the French Anglo-Arab, Connetable.

Here then we had instances of the Arab performing the finer and most elegant movements of the true riding horse in the highest degree of excellence. There are many other instances, of course, and the time may come when the Society will be able to stage dressage competitions of its own. It is known that there are many Arabians in different parts of the country qualified to compete in dressage tests, and there are a number more in various stages towards that end. It is probable that if this were organised and encouraged it would not only give much pleasure to owners, but to spectators as well. How, indeed, can the elegance and quality of the Arab be better shown than in a display of dressage, which, in itself, is a demonstration of equine elegance at its best?

That the Arab is an ideal pupil for dressage is beyond doubt, especially the stallion. Quite apart from the fact that the breed represents the true saddle-horse (and this he has been for centuries) his very intelligence makes him easy to teach. He is noted for his apparent desire to obey, and it is said by trainers of horses, particularly the 'liberty' horses of the circus ring, that where endless repetition of a particular act, or phase of an act, is required, horses of other breeds will, in those conditions, often go 'sour' and generally show some form of resistance, whereas the Arab stallion will carry on to the end. High School and dressage displays and competitions for the Arabian in our show rings could be publicity of a very high order.

Valuable publicity of another kind and, as far as I remember, unique in its conception, was given at the Society's Show at Roehampton Club in 1956, the year in which Sir Henry Abel Smith held office as President, and which was made particularly memorable by the presence of Her Majesty the Queen at the Show. For some years past a number of Arab-bred ponies had been scoring repeated successes at the more important of our shows. In the past this field had been dominated by the pony produced by the crossing of a small Thoroughbred with one or other of our Native breeds. Prominent among these were the lovely Pretty Polly, My Pretty Maid and a number of others, all claiming the same sire, Mrs S. A. Nicholson's grey Arab, Naseel, which for many years had stood at her stud in Ireland. Incidentally, apart from these ponies the remarkable Naseel had sired champion, or first prize-winning, hunters and cobs, which had won at Dublin and other shows in Ireland and elsewhere. From 1946 to 1959 Naseel sired the Champion pony at the Spring and Summer shows at Dublin seventeen times, and gained thirteen Reserve Championships. This must certainly be a record. It was Sir Henry's idea to parade Naseel with many of his sons and daughters to let the world see what an Arab could produce, and so we had a parade in the ring of a large number of ponies led by their sire Naseel. A running commentary for a thing of this sort was obviously called for, which I gave.

Something of the same sort has been an annual feature of the Society's Show. I refer, of course, to the Sire Produce Group, where the more successful progeny of certain sires are paraded in their sire-groups, the groups being in competition for the placings and awards. For certain reasons, which it seems difficult to avoid, this class always comes at the very end of the first day of the show, when the attendance tends to dwindle to somewhat meagre proportions. To my mind, from a number of viewpoints, there is no more attractive *and instructive* class to be seen than this.

A year or so later when Sir Henry was President of the Royal Windsor Horse Show, he organised another parade which was really even better publicity for the Arab breed. It was a parade of a large number of Anglo-Arab and Part-bred Arab horses and ponies, all winners of a variety of classes held at shows throughout the country and led by three of the recent Champion Arab Stallions. I was concerned with Sir Henry in the choice of these horses and ponies and it was surprising to find what a large number we had to choose from; certainly, there was no lack of 'copy' for the commentary which I gave.

CHAPTER FIVE

The True Arabian

The very essence of all horse breeding, with the exception of the racehorse, is that all progeny must conform to the breed's established or recognised type, whether this is based on what has been known as such or has evolved throughout the centuries or, as in the case of 'made' breeds, that is part-breds which have acquired a breed name, to the make and shape as decided by those who were responsible for its introduction and its subsequent standards. In either case, whatever the breed or type, adherence to this principle must obviously be the aim of the breeder, for if it is ignored neither breed nor type can hope to remain fixed. Without this essential factor any breed could, and no doubt would, in but a few generations, revert to something quite away from the type and standard intended. I should mention, however, and all who have knowledge of the breed are aware, that the ability of the Arab, whether male or female, to stamp its type on successive generations is remarkable, and its prepotency is so strong that the Arab blood becomes, to put it very simply, very hard to breed out. The Arab type tends to be visual throughout a long period even to be counted in centuries.

The importance of breeding to the highest possible standards of conformation, action and true Arabian type and character is, therefore, of even greater importance in this ancient breed, for it will be obvious that once faults are allowed to creep in, the task of breeding them out, in this prepotent breed, is a long and thankless one to say the least. How distressing to those who to-day breed, and endeavour to breed, Arabians of the highest class and as a result of their efforts find a gradual improvement in the standard of their animals, to hear remarks (and these have been made too often) to the effect that nowadays one doesn't take much notice of sickle hocks in Arabs. Or again, as was overheard recently at the Arab Show: 'You *must* have a straight profile with an Arab!' How can one hope to keep the purity and beauty of the breed if such ignorance is displayed and goes uncorrected?

What is to be said of breeders, and even judges, who tolerate the mean sloping croup or the tail set *inches* down the quarters? How many are there who take seriously the horse that is 'back of the knee', or as it is called calf-kneed, that in which the shoulder is straight, or the head too long and badly set on the neck? From this it may be thought that all these faults, one or more of which may be found in any breed, are commonly found in the Arab, but they are certainly not, although one must admit the sickle hock is found too often. I only emphasize them because they *are* to be found, and my experience leads me to the conclusion that they are all too frequently ignored, or at least treated too light-heartedly.

I am quite certain the Arab breed has suffered in the past and does so to-day because of its undoubted charm, intelligence and particularly its beauty and the romance which is attached to its very name. Its association with the Bedouin and his family in the desert and with the life of the nomad in general, with the tribal warfare and the hunting of the gazelle with the Saluki hound, as did the Bedouin in bye-gone days, have all had their influence. So many young people are obsessed with the idea of owning an Arab and some are lucky enough to do so. Adults too, similarly ignorant about the breed, acquire an Arab mare, and breed from her to the nearest and cheapest stallion, innocently enough, but perhaps with almost tragic results. This has done, and is doing, the greatest possible harm to the breed. I know these are strong words to use but it is much better to force this home to all who breed Arabs or contemplate doing so, than to shut the eye and remain silent. I am often amazed by the ignorance displayed by many in their lack of knowledge of type, and their inability to detect obvious faults in conformation.

What then should be considered the perfect Arabian Horse? For many years now the Arab Horse Society has adopted, as its guide to the true Arabian, a pamphlet written by the late Lady Wentworth which can be purchased by anyone who wishes to do so. It is known as Arabian Type and Standard. In no sense would I wish, for one moment, to attempt to impose my ideas on this, or suggest any alterations. What I would like to do is to give my own idea of what I look for in the true Arabian and how I set about either to judge it or to make a detailed report on an animal. Whatever qualifications I may have are based on the fact that I have been closely associated with the Arab for nearly 50 years. I have judged a very great many stallions, mares, geldings and young stock, ridden scores of Arab stallions and many mares, and, apart from this, visited most of the big studs here, and have made most detailed inspection reports for various reasons, and for many people, at home and abroad.

As a preliminary to what follows, I should say that whatever the ideas of the individual may be, the Council of the Society has declined to lay down any rule as to the limit of the height of the stallion or the mare. Arguments on this point flared up a few years after the Second World War, some maintaining that an Arab could grow to any size, yet not lose its true Arabian type and character. On the other hand, and undoubtedly they represented the great majority, there were those who held that to do so was to invite the straight face, the long back and the long cannon bone and the 'hocks up in the air'. In short, a general lack of the true type. This is only conjecture, but I should say there are very few to-day who favour the large Arab, and personally I can only hope they will remain few in number, or better still, change their belief in the big horse. What is the acceptable size for the Arab? I should say the stallion 14·2 to 15 h.h., the mare slightly less. One can only read with real concern stud advertisements of one standing 15·1½ h.h. at 3 years, and of another standing 15·2 h.h.

Now as to what to look for in the highest class of Arabian:
Head. This must be almost abnormally short and of great refinement, having a distinct concave or 'dished' line of face. This
is the *jibbah*; it is strictly found only in Arabs and is unique to the
breed. It refers to the bulge between the eyes up to a point between
the ears and down across the first third of the nasal bone. It is a
formation of the frontal and parietal bones and appears in the form
of a shield. It is more pronounced in young stock up to the second
year, becomes modified at maturity and is rounded and more
prominent in males. Nothing is more important than this *jibbah*,
or dish, in establishing true type. The straight face must be relentlessly penalised.

The *muzzle* must be exceptionally small and tapering to lie
snugly in the half closed hand. The nostrils must be very flexible
and when the horse is excited, especially so in the stallion, should
become greatly extended and drawn to a somewhat oblong shape.
Note here that the lips and whole muzzle surface should be of very
soft texture, somewhat akin to the flesh of a freshly picked young
mushroom; any tendency to a coarse, or rubbery, surface denotes
a lack of breeding and should be so noted.

The *eyes* must be set low in the head and widely spaced when
viewed from the front. These two points are of great, even vital,
importance, together with the fact that they cannot be too large.
Viewed from the front they should stand away from the head,
and even from behind this should be noticeable. In appearance
they must be dark and deep in colour, very soulful in the mare, in
the stallion capable in an instant of showing great alertness, with
enormous challenging dignity.

The *ears* rather long in the mare, shorter in the stallion; both
shapely, alertly carried.

Note now the *jaws*. The more they resemble the generous
roundness of the soup-plate the better (this is a striking feature
compared with other breeds of horses) and they should be capable
of receiving a large closed fist between the spread. If they will
accommodate this it denotes something very good.

We come now to the *neck*. While it is desirable to have a long neck, that is one which gives the rider a long front or 'rein', an excessively long neck, however desirable in theory, is away from type in the Arab. Better, therefore, to have a generous length of rein, which, of course, means a good long neck, provided it is not out of proportion with the horse as a whole, for such are found from time to time. Making, if necessary, due allowance for lack of condition, or as is sometimes the case, lack of strength owing to youth, it should give every indication of substance without coarseness and elegance without weakness. A good well-furnished neck is recognisable by all.

While still on the subject of the neck there is the importance of the *mitbah*, a term which is only applied to the Arab and refers to the peculiar angle at which the neck enters the head. In fact it makes (or certainly should) a slight angle at the top of the crest, and from that point runs in a gentle curve to the head. The windpipe enters the head in the same way. The more this is accentuated the greater the ability of the head to be moved freely in any direction. Before I leave the neck I will refer to the mane, the texture of which may well pass unscrutinised by most, yet should not be overlooked by the judge. The finer the hair the greater the quality and, if a comparison can be made, I should say it should be, if possible, as nearly equal in texture to the fine hair of a woman's head. It should be finer than that of any other breed, and this applies to both sexes, although that of the stallion may be slightly coarser than that of the mare.

We next come to the *body*. With this is included the shoulder, which should be well sloped, though being an Arab it will not be excessively so, for that is not typical of the breed. Note here that a good shoulder can remain undisclosed, or a bad one shown at its very best, when showing the horse in hand. The more pronounced the *wither* is in size the better. It is, however, exceptional to find these very prominent. The *back* must be very short, strong in appearance and slightly concave, with the *body* deep and markedly strong, having shapely rounded *ribs* and an ample deep *girth*.

Impari. Part-bred Arab. Bay Mare (Shifari/Impala). (Photo by Photonews)

Shammar. Grey Stallion (Champurrado/Somra II).

El Meluk. Chestnut Stallion (Mikeno/Mifaria). (Photo by Photonews)

El Meluk (left) and *Mikeno* (right). El Meluk-Chestnut Stallion
(Mikeno/Mifaria). Mikeno-Chestnut Stallion (Rissalix/Namilla).
(Photo by Monty)

Condemn the plain, that is too straight back, but make allowance for rather too much dip in the top line in the horse advanced in age and the elderly blood mare. Make no allowances for the long back and one with too much space, weakness, or obvious lack of strength between the back rib and the stifle joint. Remember that the Arab is essentially a short-backed and, therefore, short-bodied horse. The *chest* must be of the true riding horse, that is to say it must not be too broad, with legs set wide apart (a 'harness' chest) nor mean, with legs close together. It must be normal in appearance.

The *quarters* must be *very* generous in the Arab and are contained in the area lying between the rear of the flank and the root of the tail, stretching downward to the top of the *gaskin*. The *croup*, that is the upper line of the quarters to the root of the tail, must be as long as possible, and as wide and flat as it well can be, while extreme length should be sought from the point of the hip to the point of the buttock. As many Arabs fail in one or more of these, particular attention should be paid to this, pointing as it does to a falling away from the required standard of perfection.

The root of the tail should come from the croup at the extreme uppermost line, and the nearer this appears as one straight line the better. This is most characteristic of the breed at its best. Anything in the nature of sloping quarters or those lacking in generous shape and substance, with tail in consequence set low, must be counted a serious defect. The hair of the tail should be similar in texture to that of the mane. The quarters as a whole must be richly furnished, generous in size with the *gaskins* pronounced and prominent, the whole showing not the slightest sign of weakness.

The *limbs* in all horses are of great importance. In the Arab the *fore-legs* should come from the body not too far underneath the trunk nor too much in front (either can be found). The *elbows* should stand away, that is allow the fingers to slip freely between them and the trunk. The *upper arm* can hardly be too strong, prominent, nor too full of muscle. The *knee* must be flat, wide and clean and this cannot be placed too low to the ground, thus ensuring the most desirable short *cannon bones*, which must not be tied-in (cut-in) below the back of the knee. Excessive bone measurement is rarely found in the Arab, but the greater the circumference below the knee the better. The bone structure of the high-caste Arabian being superior in internal density, big bone measurement is not deemed to be of such great importance as in other breeds. It is a sign of weakness, and thus undoubtedly a fault, if the horse is calf-kneed or 'back of the knee', that is when the fore-legs, viewed from the side and having an imaginary line perpendicularly drawn through the centre, tend to concavity below the knee. The *pasterns* should be neither too long nor too upright and should join *fetlock joints* of adequate size, well shaped, clean, and showing no puffiness.

The *hind legs* must first and foremost be straight and without any indication of being sickle, bent, or cow-hocked. The former is where the whole formation of the leg viewed from the side is bent inwards, is weak looking and somewhat resembles a long drawn-out sickle in shape. The *hocks*, clean and sharply defined, must neither tend to turn outwards ('going wide-behind') nor inwards ('cow-hocked'). Of great importance, too, is the fact that the hocks, like the knees, must be placed as low as possible. If they are, this is a favourable feature making for short cannon (shannon) bones, which must not be tied, or cut-in, below the front of the hock.

The *feet* must all be level in appearance and size, being neither too spread or open, nor contracted, nor upright or 'donkey-footed'. In texture they must be hard and smooth with an absence of rings or other irregularities. They must certainly show no signs of concavity.

At the *walk* the action must be true and level, and must go neither too close nor too wide, whether in front or behind. The *trot* is one of great freedom with good use of shoulder and showing a generous stride (exaggerated action in the forelegs is out of type). Little, if any, knee action is shown and the same applies to the *canter*. The true Arabian action is very typical and unique, for it is not found in any other breed and it is finished off by a tail-carriage which is unmistakable. The root or dock is held high and, as it were, triumphantly, with the tail itself showing like a flag unfurled in the wind.

The *Arabian type* is unforgettable, being not only beautiful and full of character, but a combination of grace and refinement, of intelligence and friendliness, and in the stallion, of added dignity and courage. Those seeking the Arab of the highest caste must look for all this and must bear in mind that, apart from all else, the head must be short, tapering, dished and of fine eye, the back short, the croup high, wide and generous; the hocks straight and the limbs short. Unless these strike the eye at first glance it is certain that this Arab is not of the highest class.

Whatever I may have written above, and whatever the official Type and Standard may decree, I cannot resist giving an extract from Homer Davenport's well-known book, *My Quest of the Arabian Horse*, published in New York over sixty years ago. Davenport, an undoubted authority, wrote this vivid general description of the Arab as he knew him in the desert:

'In stature, he stands fourteen hands and two inches high and is more often a little under than over that. He is a very perfect animal; he is not large here and small there. There is a balance and harmony throughout his frame not seen in any other horse. He is the quint-essence of all good qualities in a compact form.

'The beauty of his head, ears, eyes, jaw, mouth and nostrils should be seen to be appreciated. The ears are not small, but are so perfectly shaped that they appear small. The head is short from the eye to the muzzle and broad and well developed above. The eye is peculiarly soft and intelligent with a sparkle character-istic of the breed. Yet when it lights up with excitement it does not have the strained wild look, and pained, staring expression, often seen in European horses. The nostrils, long and puckered, are drawn back and are capable of great distension. The neck is a model of length and forms a perfect arch that matches the arch of his tail. The throat is particularly large and well developed. It is loose and pliant when at rest, and much detached from the rest of the neck. This feature is not often noticed, though it is indicative not only of good wind, but of prolonged exertion without distress, owing to the great width between the jaws. The two great features, possibly, that a novice would notice quickest in the Arab horse, is the forehead, or jibbah, which cannot be too prominent, and the other is the tail set high and carried in an arch.

'The build of the Arab is perfect. It is essentially that of utility. The space for the seat of the rider at once fixes his true position and his weight is carried on that part of the frame most adapted for it. If he be carefully examined it will be found that all the muscles and limbs of progression are better placed and longer in him than in any other horse. Nature, when she made the Arab, made no mistake'.

Those simple words in the first paragraph, and indeed all that Davenport wrote, strike one as a wonderful summing up of the perfection of conformation and balance of the breed, a vivid picture of the true Arabian which surely can hardly be bettered.

Ermine Toes (Anglo-Arab). Bay Mare (Mikeno/Slipstream).

Harwood Asif. Chestnut Stallion (Zeus/Fafika). (Photo by Photonews)

Karramba. Grey Mare (Witraz/Karmen II). Bred in Poland. (Photo by Photonews)

Argos. Grey Stallion (Nabor/Arfa). Bred in Poland. (Photo by John Nestle)

Gerwazy. Grey Stallion (Doktryner/Gwara). Bred in Poland. (Photo by Photonews)

Trypolitanka. Bay Mare (Trypolis/Eleonora).

Kossak. Chestnut Stallion (Rushti/Karramba).

Nerinora. Chestnut Mare (Oran/Nerina). (Photo by John Nestle)

CHAPTER SIX

The Arab for Sale

The subject matter of this chapter may well look a little strange and out of place considering the title of this book, but I am convinced that what I write under this heading is of far more importance to the Arab owner and breeder than most imagine, if indeed they give any thought to it at all.

The days of the big horse-dealers in this country are a thing of the past. At the close of the last century, and for a number of years after, they were to be found literally all over the country, as well as a number of small ones. None was much concerned, however, with the Arab breed for the obvious reason so few were for sale. To-day, on account of the number of Arabs here, quite a surprising number change hands both in the form of home sales and for export. Why and how do these take place?

The 'whys' are fairly obvious, yet a little analysis can be of interest. Ever since I can remember imports of the breed have been very few in number and have now virtually ceased, and I can see no reason why they are ever likely to play any important part, certainly not those from the Arabian desert. It may be in view of the excellence of the breed in the United States of America and the numbers to be found there, we may find ourselves even importing from there, perhaps to renew some particular blood strain. From this I exclude the import of the Polish-Arab, having dealt with these at some length in Chapter 8, 'Our Immigrants'. This is a recent but a very important factor in the scheme of things. Besides the Polish Arab we have imported a few Russian Arabs which may also make some impact on the home studs. Nonetheless, the breeder in England has to look at home to improve his stock in most instances.

Apart from general stud improvement, where a stallion and several mares are the property of one owner, it becomes almost inevitable that the need to get rid of the former eventually becomes almost imperative, owing to the stud becoming saturated with the blood of this one particular horse. A new horse *must* be found to save the expense, not to mention the time and trouble, involved in sending the home mares away for service to new blood.

Probably the most frequent reason for seeking a market is the urgent need to dispose of surplus colts. Take the case of a stud which has perhaps ten to a dozen mares and unkind fate decides that among the new season's foal-crop eight or nine are colts. A pretty problem then presents itself, even if the number should be no more than half a dozen. No one wants to geld an Arab, though it would often be far better for the breed were this done more frequently. The price factor too has much to do with this, as there is generally a wide difference between the price of a good gelding and even an indifferent colt.

There are too many who will buy an indifferent entire knowing that, apart from his own one or two mares, he can be used on a few mares in the neighbourhood and so earn some fees to help with the over-heads. These fees, which in the early days were often no higher than five guineas, are now often 15 to 25 guineas, or even more, for something no one could be very proud to own and should certainly not breed from. This, of course, is just another instance of the popularity of the breed. Far too many are inclined to breed, irrespective of true type and conformation. How often one hears it said 'ever since I was a child I have dreamed of having an Arab and now at last . . . .

It is generally admitted that too much in-breeding is taking place to-day so that, apart from the stallion owner finding he needs another horse for his mares, many mare owners fight shy of a horse and his progeny which are beginning to get the reputation of being used too much and whose blood is too wide-spread about the country.

There is also another reason for selling. Disappointments often arise as the result of home-breeding, or perhaps in gambling in the purchase of something very young. Whether male or female, the conclusion is arrived at that to keep this young thing is just not going to do the stud any good. The decision to sell, in this case, therefore is wise and usually I should be all in favour of it being carried out, for we should all strive for perfection. Just bear in mind, however, that the growing Arab is sometimes a peculiar and unpredictable animal and round about the ages of two and three, great changes can, and often do, take place; for the better, usually, thank goodness. Don't be too hasty; remember there are many breeders of long experience who probably would be glad to advise. Necks can grow longer, eyes become larger, quarters become more generous and tails start to be carried higher. This is not as silly as it sounds and one should always seek expert advice, for it is surprising what changes can take place in a matter of months. In such cases it is wise to consider the pedigree carefully. There is no doubt that some breed-lines are very slow in developing and in such cases it is wise to consider the pedigree carefully before making a decision. Ugly ducklings can delight their owners by becoming elegant swans, and that by the way is no great exaggeration.

The greatest reason to sell is, however, really over-stocking of our usually all too limited acreages and particularly overstocking with colts. Every stud owner knows this can become a most embarrassing, not to say a serious, matter.

Once the decision to sell is reached the only question then to be resolved is how it is to be done.

It has been a feature for many years now at the Society's Annual Show to hold an Auction Sale which is obviously as potentially a satisfactory means to secure a good sale as any, for here is assembled the largest number of Arab breeders and owners (actual and potential) to be found during the course of the year. Held, as it is, at the very end of July, however, on the threshold

51

of Autumn with the long winter ahead, most prospective buyers may well hesitate before taking on another horse in the stable, remembering grazing days are nearly over and that it will be a good six months before the new grass will be available. Unless the animal is for some particular reason of exceptional interest, the seller may well decide to postpone the sale until the spring or, alternatively, not wait for the show but seek other and earlier means to find a buyer.

There are other periodical Auction Sales of mixed breeds held in the country, but it is very doubtful whether they offer a satisfactory centre for either the seller or buyer of Arabs. That being so the best medium may be found to be advertising. We have, fortunately, a satisfactory medium in the paper *Horse & Hound*, and there are other horse papers covering a large potential market. The Society itself does what it can to help the seller through the advertising pages of the issues of the official journal, *The Arab Horse News*. Unfortunately, the number of these published throughout the year is limited. The Society keep, for the benefit of its members, a current Sales Register which is of great use to those either buying or selling. Beyond all this is the very considerable number of sales which take place between breeders and owners who, by their grape-vine, get to know what is for sale. Next to our weekly *Horse and Hound* probably the greatest number of sales take place in this way.

How about the remunerative export sales? It is really very hard to give a reliable opinion on this point. There is no doubt much help is to be had from those here who have sold abroad animals *which have given complete satisfaction*. Such people if unable to satisfy enquiries themselves, often pass on the enquiry. Confidence breeds assurance and the integrity of those concerned is vital and something to treasure. A certain amount of advertising of English Arabs in the American papers takes place, but with what success I wouldn't like to say.

At the present time there is a large potential and unsatisfied market for good Arabs and this looks like lasting for a considerable time. It would be unwise to be too optimistic about this, but anyone who owns a really good mare and has the facilities for breeding should not hesitate to do so, for there is a ready sale of fillies.

It is of interest to mention here, and it may come as a surprise to many, that there are probably not less than 200 Studs of Arabian horses in England, most of them very small it is true; in fact, it is said that the average number of inmates is no higher than three, while perhaps only six studs have more than 20. In so small a country it is remarkable that so many breeding establishments are to be found. Maybe this can be looked upon as a satisfactory feature, for the concentration of so many in so small an area must surely encourage sales, interchanging of blood and, beyond anything perhaps, stimulating interest in the breed.

CHAPTER SEVEN

The Question of Breed Improvement

The difficult question as to whether the breed has improved over the years is often asked, and to answer it one must consider the Arab as it has been bred in Great Britain during the present century. This at once raises a difficulty, for how many are there alive to-day who have known the breed over the greater portion of that period? Again, and even less helpful, is the fact that there were, in the early part of the century, but few Arabs in the country as compared with the number to-day. Crabbet Park Stud was started by Wilfrid Scawen Blunt and Lady Anne Blunt, the parents of Lady Wentworth, and until the death of the latter in 1957 it remained the biggest stud in the country. The only other stud comparable in type and numbers was that of H. V. Musgrave Clark, which he founded in 1900, and which has enjoyed for sixty-six years the enviable reputation for breeding Arabs to the type originally imported by the Blunts from the desert. Let these, the Crabbet and the Courthouse Arabs be the criterion on which to make comparison, to try, in fact, to discover whether the years have shown improvement or otherwise.

Many years ago I was watching the judging of the class for Arabs under saddle at the Royal International at the White City with Ernest E. Hutton, now a veteran horseman of some 90 years, and whom I look upon as one of the best informed to-day on the greatest number of breeds throughout the world. He remarked that no breed had shown greater improvement than the Arab. Shortly after this I asked Musgrave Clark his opinion, and he said that *on the whole* the breed had *not* improved.

No truly pure breed is capable of improvement in the strict sense, least of all the ancient Arabian, for alien blood is unknown; indeed, should it be introduced, the result is that it at once becomes either Anglo-Arab or Part-bred Arab. The reverse, however, is true of all the 'made' breeds which can, and have been time without number, fortified and improved by the introduction of alien blood mostly through the Arab and/or Thoroughbred. On this subject of improvement I will quote from a speech made at Crabbet Park on 5th July, 1902, by Wilfrid Scawen Blunt:

'It was the conviction that this wonderful breed of horses was threatened with extinction in its native home that led me, 25 years ago, to make the attempt you now see carried out at Crabbet of rescuing at least a fraction of the race and preserving it in all its purity in England. This was my first and most important object —*not to improve the breed*—for it really needs no improvement— but to keep it pure; pure not only in blood, but in type also, to preserve it carefully from deterioration in shape, in temper, in hardihood, and from departure from those special characteristics of beauty which are peculiar to the ancient race'.

My great hope is that all breeders shall hold these words of Scawen Blunt as sacred, as I have most certainly done in all my writings and all my judgings of the breed.

That these were enormously important words need no emphasis. That no breeder of the Arab Horse to-day should ever forget this dictum is vital to the welfare of the breed for all time. There is only one way the Arab can be improved and that is by selective breeding within the breed itself, to which much careful thought must be given. The best stallion must be used which is likely to eliminate faults, improve such as are capable of improvement and achieve the over-all aim of producing the ideal type as suggested by the produce of the above studs. Have our breeders over the years retained this standard or allowed a certain recession to take charge? In the answer to this (if it can be found) is the answer to the question asked in this chapter.

While suggesting, truthfully enough, that those best able to answer the question are those who knew the Arab forty, fifty and more years ago, it may be some help to remind the present generation of breeders of the names of some of the winning sires and dams since the war, for many of them will have been seen in the flesh. The following are the winners of the five years and over class for stallions (in 1963 this class was altered to six years old and over):

1948	Lady Wentworth's Raktha.	1956	Lady Wentworth's Grand Royal.
1949	Mrs H. V. M. Clark's Rashid.	1957	Lady Wentworth's Indian Magic.
1950	Lady Wentworth's Dargee.	1958	C. G. Covey's Silver Vanity.
1951	Lady Wentworth's Dargee.	1959	C. G. Covey's Bright Shadow.
1952	H. V. M. Clark's Bahram.	1960	C. G. Covey's Dargee.
1953	Lady Wentworth's Grand Royal.	1961	Mrs H. Linney's Mikeno.
		1962	Crabbet Stud's Silver Vanity.
1954	H. V. M. Clark's Bahram.	1963	H. V. M. Clark's Benjamin.
1955	Lady Wentworth's Dargee.	1964	H. V. M. Clark's Shammar.
		1965	J. Alexander's Argos.

A glance at the above will show that the winners were to be found amongst no more than four studs, for the names of Lady Wentworth, C. G. Covey and Crabbet are synonymous with Crabbet Park. However, this has no particular bearing on the question under discussion. What is pertinent, for all who would form their own opinion, is to consider their trueness to type and correctness of conformation.

We are, when talking of breeding, a little inclined, perhaps, to consider the stallion as all important, relegating the mare somewhat to the background. This is wrong, of course, and while I do not intend to discuss in detail the importance of the distaff side, it is necessary to look at the mares in the same way as we looked at the sires. I give a list of the winning brood mares in the four years old and upwards class:

1948	Lady Wentworth's Grey Royal.	1957	Lady Wentworth's Silver Diamond.
1949	G. H. Ruxton's Algoletta.	1958	Mrs A. M. Roberts' Ambria.
1950	Lady Wentworth's Rissiletta.	1959	C. G. Covey's Sirella.
1951	Lady Wentworth's Silver Shadow.	1960	Miss M. Evans, Eloia.
1952	Lady Wentworth's Shades of Night.	1961	Crabbet Stud's Wentworth Golden Shadow.
1953	Lady Wentworth's Silver Shadow.	1962	Crabbet Stud's Sirella.
1954	Mrs E. M. Murray's Shallufah.	1963	Major & Mrs Hedley's Samaveda.
1955	Thriplow Farm's Ghayran.	1964	Crabett Stud's Nerinora.
1956	Lady Wentworth's Silver Shadow.	1965	Mr & Mrs Dinsdale's Lilac Domino.

It will be noted that the mares are concentrated in very few studs to much the same extent as were the stallions. Viewed together, stallions and mares, how good are the present-day representatives? It will be realised, of course, that all the above are winners at the premier Arab show in England and, it may be fairly claimed, in the world, although the U.S.A. have many Arabians of the very highest class, especially among the mares. It would not, however, give a fair picture to decide on the basis of a few of the best of those years.

The list of Arabs at stud for 1966 as advertised in the Society's publication is given as 77. It is difficult to say how many more there are which are not offered to the public for this purpose, but it is certain that the total number of stallions is considerably in excess of 100. There are, too, many which were then too young to qualify as stallions. How many females of all ages there are I would not like to say. One thing is certain, in our world of horses in Great Britain, the Arabian holds a position of great importance. What breed if any, except the racehorse, ranks higher in point of average value? Such being the case, what sort of stock are they producing? We need to get at an over-all or cross-section of the Arabian population to arrive at an Equine Gallup Poll! In the absence of one, and we must accept the fact that we are a long way off from Gallup Polls, this may be of some guide.

For various reasons I have over the last several years received from many parts of the world, as well as from home sources, many requests for advice from those wanting to buy or sell Arabs; general advice about a stud or some particular stallion or mare, and where such can be found that is for sale; what to ask for this or that horse; whether a certain price asked is justified and so on. After visiting many establishments I found that, for the satisfaction of all concerned, some ordered form of inspection and particularly a summary was essential, and so I evolved an inspection form with a summary.

I most strongly recommend that something of this sort should be used by all enthusiasts; it can be most illuminating. If the comments are given accurately with knowledge and sense, the result is most valuable, for within these limits the picture that appears will be a fair and honest one. Here is what I comment on:
Colour: Height: Markings: Head: Eyes: Ears: Jowl: Neck: Withers: Shoulder: Back: Body: Girth: Ribs: Chest: Quarters: Tail: Arms: Knees: Cannon Bone: Elbows: Croup: Hip to Buttock: Gaskins: Hocks: Pasterns: Limbs: Feet: Action: Temperament: Type: Quality: Easy to catch? Traffic shy? If shown—successes and where?

Needless to say the resulting information is of great interest for reference and can be of real value. I seem to remember Lady Wentworth telling me she always noted, in a little book which she carried, a commentary on any horse she had a chance really to look at.

The result on all my findings on each horse inspected have given me more than 150 detailed reports. The subjects under scrutiny range from the indifferent, not to say bad animals, to the really high class. The prices vary greatly and this, of course, is influenced by the age of the animal and the need of the seller to sell, or sometimes even the anxiety of the buyer to buy. Obviously the main factor is the true worth of the animal. Incidentally, my many inspections have included a number of Arabs which I have not thought worthy of detailed reports, and some good ones which were not really what I knew the prospective buyer was seeking.

Looking critically at my files from the point of view of prices only, I must say the market over the last few years has most certainly been a seller's one. Three, four and five hundred guineas for colts, and in exceptional cases up to 1,000 guineas even for yearlings and more for varying ages, while I notice 1,750 guineas for a young mare, the same for a five-year-old stallion and again the same refused for a two-year-old filly. All this points to the satisfactory state of Arab breeding, whether for moderate or exceptionally good stock.

Every horse can be faulted, or should I say *practically* every one, but I think the first is more accurate. In consequence it follows that of the many hundreds I have inspected, or merely 'looked at', and of the hundreds I have judged, I have to admit I have seen many faults. Had I been doing the same with any other breed I have no doubt that the ratio of faults would have been much the same, Thoroughbreds not excepted, which is natural enough, for in the main they are bred entirely for speed on the racecourse. With all these observations in mind, with the names of the winners previously mentioned (including the thousands I have seen at shows), and not forgetting Ernest Hutton's and Musgrave Clark's views, what is *my* opinion? Price alone can be very misleading, especially as there has been so large an increase in recent years.

Some years ago I wrote in my *Lifetime With Horses*: 'I can't speak with personal knowledge of Crabbet Park as it was in the early days of this century, but Musgrave Clark can, and he tells me that there is nothing to-day to compare with the overall true Arabian type which he knew there in the days of Lady Anne

Blunt. This may well be so and I certainly can't dispute it. I can, however, say that during the last twenty years I have seen many Arabians which left much to be desired. On the other hand there are many beautiful and typical Arabians to be seen in studs up and down the country and because of this, Ernest Hutton may be right in calling attention to the great improvement, but I can't help feeling that they were probably better sixty years ago. I know from judging and inspecting scores of them how difficult it is to find many Arabs of the highest class to-day with faultless hind-legs.

To this I would add it seems increasingly difficult to find the really short head tapering to the very small muzzle and the high, flat and broad croup. I wrote that it is 'increasingly hard', but it may be that it appears so because there are so many more Arabs in the country. Be that as it may, I feel that what I have quoted above remains my opinion with this important corollary: A few to-day compare most favourably with those of the past and may well be superior, but that the majority compare unfavourably.

I ask any serious student of the breed—*do our average stallions and mares live up to the type of those shown in so many pictures of the Arab of the desert* and his white-robed attendant, the very epitome of nobility, grace and courage, his great challenging eyes and flaring nostrils, a challenge to all?

CHAPTER EIGHT

Our Immigrants

Over the centuries the source from which practically all Arabs in this country came from was Arabia, although from time to time they found their way here from other countries. Of these latter some had their origin in the Arabian Desert while others were bred in the country from which they were imported. Undoubtedly the main source of the breed, as it is constituted in England to-day, was the Crabbet Arabian Stud in Sussex, founded at the end of the last century by Wilfrid Scawen Blunt and his wife Lady Anne Blunt. They in turn had established the Sheykh Obeid Stud in Egypt in 1879, and from time to time transferred horses from there to Crabbet Park. The majority of Arabs to be found in the country to-day have Crabbet blood. It can be asserted with some confidence that, so far as numbers are concerned, importations of Arabs from the desert during the first half of this century have been very few.

Mention must be made of a horse of rare quality and one outstandingly successful as a sire—Skowronek. This grey horse by Ibrahim out of Jaskotka was bred on the borders of Poland in 1909 and was imported by Walter Winans, it has been said, mainly because of its beauty. Perhaps this was literally true, for Winans (an American by birth though living at the time in England) was a sculptor of considerable renown. The bronze statue by him of Skowronek is in the possession of Musgrave Clark, and to the latter must go the credit of securing this horse for breeding in this country. It is interesting to recall the fact that on the memorable occasion of the opening of the International Horse Show at Olympia in 1907, which received enormous support from America both financially and otherwise, the number of entries made by Walter Winans exceeded all others. He was something of a specialist in many breeds of horses and variety seems to have appealed to him particularly.

Skowronek was not long in Winans' possession, however, for he passed into the hands of Musgrave Clark, one of the most knowledgeable and astute of Arab breeders. There he remained for some years and proved a very successful sire; apart from his other virtues, he remains in Musgrave Clark's memory as a horse of outstandingly charming temperament. Skowronek, however, was to find another home, for his owner was persuaded to part with him under great pressure (and it seems some misunderstanding) to Lady Wentworth. Crabbet Park then became this grey stallion's last home. No student of the pedigree of Arabs over the last fifty years need be reminded of the influence for good left by this importation from Poland, a country having an outstanding reputation for good horse-breeding.

During the many years which followed I can recall no importations of Arabs of any note either from Poland or elsewhere until 1959. In that year, however, the Arab breeders in this country and probably in the United States, too, were considerably surprised, to say the least, to learn that five Arab mares had arrived at the London Docks from Poland. Little did anyone realise that this, the inaugural shipment of Polish-bred Arabians to this country, was merely the forerunner of many more from the same source. What has been the impact of this sudden and almost alarming intrusion of the Polish-Arab on the home product? What will future breeding uncover? Has it been a wise move, this introduction of fresh blood to the English Arabian?

In the very centre of England there lives an enthusiastic young breeder of Arabs, Miss Patricia Lindsay. Possessed of undoubted ability, great enthusiasm for the breed, of high intellect and a gay and charming personality, Patricia Lindsay is a considerable linguist and among other languages she learnt Polish. Armed with this and a burning enthusiasm she set off, without any official encouragement, to investigate the Arab in Poland, and it was on her own responsibility that the shipment referred to arrived at London. Later three more visits were made and twelve more Arabs were imported. Every one of these horses, three stallions and colts, 14 mares and fillies, was duly inspected and entered in the Stud Book of the Arab Horse Society. It is interesting to record their names as some have attained considerable fame. In 1959 came the following mares: The bay, Celina, the greys, Czantoria, Karramba, Carmencita, and the chestnut, Damietta.

Later in the same year a grey stallion and a brown mare arrived —Gerwazy and Gehenna; while late in December a bay colt, Grojec, and a grey mare, Latawica, were imported, while two stallions and six mares went to the U.S.A.

In June, 1961, the grey mare, Lafirynda, arrived, and she was followed by three more mares, the bay, Mufta, and two greys, Navarra and Chimera, and a grey stallion, Argos. In 1963, two grey mares, Barcelona and Biruta, and a bay, Almaviva, completed the importations up to that date.

Somewhat later than these earlier visits of Miss Lindsay's, Dr H. C. E. M. Houtappel of the Rodania Arabian Stud of Laren, Holland, undertook similar journeyings to Poland with the result that his Stud became possessed of several Polish Arabians, amongst them, Elzunia, a beautiful mare and full sister to Musgrave Clark's Celina, which I have already mentioned, and a bay mare, Trypolitanka, which was later imported into England and became the property of Leslie Theobald, M.R.C.V.S., of Stafford, for whom she has produced some exceptionally good foals. Since the arrival of Patricia Lindsay's first Arabs from Poland, 17 have been imported and at a rough guess there are now perhaps 30 of their progeny in the country, some pure Polish, others part Polish and part English. I think this is an outstanding fact.

Such sudden and almost violent introduction of new blood, however purely Arabian it might be, produced understandable doubts and criticisms. Whether these have been justified or not, those who have now made personal acquaintance with the new-comers, or seen some of the many photographs which have been published, will have formed their own opinion. Whether they have decided to praise or condemn, it is certainly worthy of note that Musgrave Clark, oldest surviving breeder of Arabs in this country, was at the dockside when the first ship tied up. He bought Celina there. Other well-known breeders have acquired Polish Arabs; for instance, Lady Anne Lytton bought the exceptionally good young bay horse, Grojec, by Comet out of Gastromonia, and won the class for four to five year olds at the Society's Show; James Alexander had the outstanding grey stallion, Argos, by one of Poland's best known stallions, Nabor, who is now in the U.S.A. Mrs A. J. Sellar obtained the grey mare, Barcelona, who produced a colt foal by Comet shortly after arrival. This colt, Cyrasa, later passed into the ownership of Leslie Theobald, and still later joined Celina at the Courthouse Stud. He is now at the New South Wales Stud in Australia. Mrs E. M. Murray bought the brown mare, Gehenna; the Marchioness Townshend of Raynham, the grey mares, Nawarra, Chimera and Czantoria (formerly owned by Patricia Lindsay, for whom she produced Chukran by Ger-wazy, a champion in U.S.A.). Major and Mrs Hedley acquired Mufta; Lady Moyne, Biruta; while Carmencita (now in U.S.A.) was owned by the late Miss M. Lyon. I think it is important to give the names of many of these Polish-Arabians for they and their stock will certainly figure prominently in the years to come in the Stud Books of the English and American Arab Horse Societies.

Such a formidable list of prominent breeders suggests that the Polish Arabian has made a very considerable impact on English studs—a remarkable state of affairs and entirely due to Patricia Lindsay. To show that these breeders are not alone in their belief in the Arab from Poland, it is estimated that their counterparts in the United States have imported some 50 animals, including Muzulmanin (out of Mufta), the biggest U.S. prize-winner in 1963, and Bask, the 1964 U.S. National Champion. Many Polish-

Blue Domino. Chestnut Stallion (Rissalix/Niseyra). (Photo by Miles Bros.)

Rajmek. Chestnut Stallion (Mikeno/Rajjela).

Blue Magic. Chestnut Stallion (Blue Domino/Indian Starlight).

Grojec. Bay Stallion (Comet/Gastronomia). (Photo by John Nestle)

Count D'Orsaz. Chestnut Stallion (Rissalix/Shamna).

Kilbees Royal Return. Part-bred Arab. Chestnut Mare (Grand Royal/-Grayling). (Photo by J. E. L. Mayes)

Bright Shadow. Chestnut Stallion (Radi/Pale Shadow). (Photo by John Nestle)

Count Ambrino. Chestnut Stallion (Count D'Orsaz/Ambria). (Photo by Photonews)

Arabians were exported direct by Patricia Lindsay for American breeders at their own request.

Soon after their arrival these Polish-bred horses made their appearance in the show ring and they have ever since been shown in good numbers. I have the impression, however, that our judges have not been too generous when making their awards. It is true that Musgrave Clark's Celina was made Champion Mare the first time shown, and that Grojec was 'recognised' and placed first in the four and five year old class, but there are a number of others which I am sure have not received their due.

Just to mention a few of these, we have the grey mare Karramba, a lovely brood mare indeed, who had to wait four years before she was placed first; Trypolitanka, who was just nowhere until she stood second at Richmond Royal Show in 1964; Argos, obviously a very fine Arab, was certainly not recognised for some time, and as for Gerwazy, I wondered when the judges would recognize his quite splendid front, his wealth of bone, his high set croup and tail and really straight hind legs.

When considering the merits of the Polish Arab vis-à-vis its English equivalent, it is worth touching on the colour question. As we all know, the predominance of the chestnut in Great Britain is now startingly evident. An analysis of the Polish-breds imported to England reveals that only one was a chestnut, and furthermore, among the remainder, there are some good dark bays, a colour which is to-day not easily found. I consider this fact to be one of the advantages which the Polish Arab has accorded us.

Questions arise in the minds of all serious breeders as to why new blood was introduced to the now well-established breed in England? Was there any call for this big invasion? Was there anything wrong in the breed to call for this, anything lacking, any loss of type? My answer to this must, of course, be taken as a purely personal one.

To a noticeable extent there is too much top-class blood confined to too few stallions, there are too few classic Arabian heads, and too few having those great prominent eyes so characteristic of the Arab from the desert. There are too many sloping quarters and croups which lack strength and breadth, and too many sickle hocks, and we musn't forget that the cannon bone cannot be too short! That is a formidable list, and under no circumstances must it be taken as a sweeping condemnation: not at all. There are many beautiful Arabs in the country which will hold their own in any company; nonetheless, there are many which have one or more of the above defects, and some are too big and so are *away from the true type*. The Arab without the true classic type of head and quarters is really not an Arab worthy of that high distinction. Criticism, if justified, must never be condemned.

If all this be true, in whatever degree, of the English horse, how can his brother from Poland implement this, or can he? The impression I have formed of the imported animal is that there is to some extent a variation in type which is hard to define. In early youth I find some are on the plain side, being late developers, but some are of marked beauty and elegance more approximating to the Arab of the desert as painted by so many artists in bygone days. My impression is of hard, sound horses with exceptionally good limbs, and croups and quarters of considerable scope, horses clean and sound and as, almost without exception, all stallions have been raced and passed the test of soundness, one would hardly expect otherwise. Such being the case it would seem that, judiciously selected, a Polish horse would be more likely than not to eliminate an obvious fault, or at any rate establish some improvement.

I suppose it is natural enough to criticise any marked innovation, and I am not immune from this by any means. I have, however, so often met with adverse comments about this or that horse, of whatever breed, without any justification at all and when one asks why, so often an answer is made which doesn't stand up to facts and sometimes even to common sense. One hears doubts expressed about the purity of the Polish-bred. Unless such doubts can be established no one has any right to mention it. If a breed is accepted for entry in the appropriate Stud Book, as of course (subject to inspection) are the Polish Arabs, it must be accepted and left at that.

Before this chapter is closed we must consider for a moment our other immigrant, the Russian Arabian, of which a few have been imported and some passed for entry in the Stud Book. I have inspected only a few of these and so am hardly qualified to express any definite opinion, but on the whole the Russians are characterised by good fronts and somewhat sloping croups. The picture I have in mind is of an exceptionally useful and hard type of horse, somewhat away from the true Arabian, yet giving the impression of a really sound animal which could be used with advantage on any mare of riding type.

According to my information there have been imported at the date of writing about 18 Russian stallions, some of which have since been gelded and some refused registration. Also there are some dozen or more mares. Of these I have seen three which pleased me very much. Can we use both the Polish and the Russian, or don't we want either?

CHAPTER NINE

Camera Studies

No matter what the medium chosen for sale may be, whether in the Press, by Stud cards, or in correspondence between breeders and owners, I consider the availability of good photographs to be of the utmost importance. In the course of the year I receive scores of letters from people asking for help to find an Arab. I look upon the ability of the seller to produce a *really* good photograph as being of great assistance. Of course, no one can expect this to sell the animal straight away, but if it is a good photograph of a good horse, the seller is much more than half way to making a sale. This sounds an extravagant statement, but after all it is only reasonable to assume that the sight of a good horse at once catches the eye of the discerning buyer, and stimulates interest. This is particularly so in the case of the overseas buyer, of whom a number buy without ever seeing the horse, as I know from personal experience. Of course, I don't mean to say that the photo begins and ends the deal, but it probably makes for more than a good start. On the other hand if it is a bad one it will probably put the buyer right off.

We are fortunate at having at our major shows not only skilled, but very helpful, professional photographers of horses. Everyone should, if possible, have a picture taken of their exhibits at various ages, and I don't mean a photograph of the moving horse or one standing in the line at a show with other horses; these are of very little value for selling or advertising purposes. What the potential buyer wants is a 'square-on' photograph of the horse looking ahead with each leg standing clear, the traditional 'English' photo-

Dolphin Play (Anglo–Arab). Bay Mare (Shifari/Bold Hart). (Photo by John Nestle)

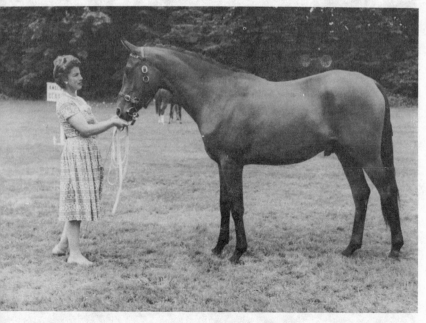

Dil Bahadur (Anglo–Arab). Bay Stallion (Shifari/Bold Hart). (Photo by Photonews)

Dancing Instructor (Anglo-Arab). Brown Stallion (Manto/Dark Continent). (Photo by Photonews)

Grey Owl. Grey Stallion (Raseem/Naxima).

graph of a horse, and these professional photographers know just how to do this and welcome the opportunity.

A prospective buyer should be given what he wants; an up-to-date photograph and any others that are available during the horse's life up to maturity. A record of pictures of this sort taken at various ages, from a week or so after foaling up to four or five years, after which very little change takes place, can be immensely rewarding and of great value to the breeder. Every point of development, good or bad, can be noticed, and all changes for the better or worse noted. That all this is of great educational value and of absorbing interest is certain, yet in spite of this most obvious comment, I cannot recall more than a few breeders who have made any attempt to record their horses seriously and regularly with first rate photographs.

Among these few I number the late Lady Wentworth, who photographed a great number at Crabbet Park, and as she was undoubtedly the greatest Arab propagandist of all time I think we can assume she considered this an important part of her ceaseless efforts in the cause of the Arabian Horse, and Crabbet Park in particular. It is worth mentioning, although I must confess this is hearsay, that many of her really successful pictures were taken with a box ('Brownie') camera! But perhaps the younger generation of breeders have never seen one—it cost but a few shillings in pre-war days.

What are needed are pictures that can be reproduced in the press, on stud cards, to illustrate articles in *The Arab Horse News*, for advertisements, or in Show reports. There is just nothing to stimulate immediate interest and invite enquiries, or to encourage a visit better than a good photograph. A good picture of a bad horse will not sell it, except to the innocents, but a good one of a good horse may well mean a sale if the price is a fair one. It may be that the stud owner does not show, or shows but very little, and so cannot get photographs taken as I have suggested. In that case the photographer to the local press, who is usually a free lance, or any other professional, so far as that goes, might be employed, as those who do this work are almost invariably possessed of excellent cameras.

The horse should stand square-on to the photographer, the head held loosely with longish rein, so that the neck is extended and so that the person holding the horse can be cut out of the picture if necessary. Pictures can be taken from either side, but with Arabs it is better from the 'off', as the mane of the Arab usually adds much charm and will probably lie on that side. The near foreleg must be forward, the near hind somewhat back, which usually sets the other two correctly, but the horse must stand *truly balanced on all four legs*. He must never stand on three feet and on the toe of the fourth. He must be alert, look straight ahead and have his ears pricked. The head must be at the full stretch of the neck without the nose being pointed forwards or tucked-in, and it must be neither held low nor high. In the final result the horse must be seen to be standing happily, balanced and poised.

There are one or two other points which should be considered by those who include photographs on stud cards, advertisements, or as auxiliaries to a sale. What is the use of showing the head only, whether taken full-face or side-face? Does it suggest that this is the horse's best feature, and that a picture of the whole may draw attention to something which is better not to emphasise? Incidentally, of what good is a gambolling foal or the rearing stallion, to advertise a stud?

What a pity it is, when pictures are shown of a horse standing square, the legs properly placed, the whole thing is spoiled by the head being slung round with the horse looking straight at the photographer. If it is happily possessed of a face with a distinct concave line, it can't be seen. No profile can be seen at all, which at once raises a suspicion that there is, if the truth were told, in fact no dish in the face line at all, and, of course, there is no sign of the all important *jibbah*. With that same poise of head what becomes of the *mitbah*, which is typical of the angle at which the neck enters the classic Arabian head? If it is there it cannot be seen, nor, for the same reason, can the refined and most desired, small muzzle of the true Arabian be discovered; it may be there or it may not. The best that can be said of the horse that looks into the face of the photographer is that it does show the breadth between the eyes and the set of these in the face, both points of prime importance to the breed.

On a recent visit to France, where I visited the famous Government Stud of Anglo-Arabs at Pompadour and certain Arab enthusiasts, I took with me a good selection of photographs of Arabs at various ages. They proved to be very good ambassadors.

If proof of what I have written is required, I would draw attention to the fact that during the course of a year *Horse and Hound* publish hundreds of photographs of Thoroughbred racehorses standing at stud. My impression is that it would be hard to find any of them which were not standing square on correctly placed legs and looking straight ahead. It is, therefore, fair to assume that all the owners are anxious to show the horse at its best, whether for stud or sale, and so they do the correct thing. If this is good enough for the bloodstock world it should be good enough for the Arab.

CHAPTER TEN

Exports

I have mentioned several times the importance of the export trade which has played so large a part in the general economics of breeders throughout the period of the Society's existence. Before then it is doubtful whether it was of any particular moment. I have pointed out that there are over 100 pure-bred Arabian stallions in the country to-day, of which 77 are offered to the public at stud. It is difficult to estimate the number of pure-bred mares and fillies in the country to-day, but it is put roughly at 1,200. There may be more, it is unlikely there are less, and the annual intake for registration shows a steady average increase. There are, of course, the obvious wastages each year owing to old age and other causes, but the resulting picture which emerges is of steadily increasing population of Arabian horses. I will not concern myself in this chapter with Anglo- and Part-bred Arabs.

What becomes of the large influx of young stock each year, this flow of pure-bred Arabians? It would certainly seem that *up to the present time* the home market is able to absorb all the young stock which breeders do not wish to keep. How true this has been over recent years only those know who have set out to buy, and this applies to the purchase of males as well as females, and of more or less any age. Any prospective purchaser will find that to buy something *really good* will entail a long search which may well prove to be a fruitless one. Breeders in this country are pretty knowledgeable and unless the buyer is prepared to pay a full price, his time and trouble will be wasted. Such is the happy position (for the seller) in the home market at the present time.

It is the same with the export market which asks for a generally higher standard of horse, commanding, naturally, a higher figure. This market, over quite a number of years now, has been excellent in the United States, in spite of efforts to restrict the import of stallions to that country. It should be noted, however, that the restrictions placed on the shipment of horses to Australia, New Zealand and all countries in the East, a restriction which prohibits their passing through the Suez Canal, has not encouraged buyers in those countries, necessitating as it does a journey round the Cape or through the Panama Canal. Buyers in these countries can, of course, obtain stock if they are prepared to face the heavier cost of air transport, a method now used with increasing frequency.

We seem now to be in the happy position of finding a market for all Arabs that become available, and this includes sub-standard horses too. Could any breeder or seller wish for more? Is any breed more happily placed, especially as prices are ruling higher to-day than ever before? The Arab sells like hot-cakes and riding as he does on the crest of the wave, how soon will the inevitable decline come, and by this I mean how soon will the seller's market turn into a buyer's? If this latter market comes about, will breeding activities have to be cut down?

No one can say when this will take place, but take place it will, there can be no doubt about that. It may occur to some, as it does to me, that the number of living Arabian horses, whatever it may be, is a high one having regard to the number of breeders and owners in so small a country as Great Britain, and, of course, apart from actual numbers, breeders are likely to find themselves continuously waging war with rising costs causing them to reduce the scale of breeding. It is sincerely to be hoped such a state of affairs will be long delayed.

In this country we are never allowed to forget that Britain must 'export or bust.' In the Arab world although such an untidy end need not be too seriously considered, it does make one wonder whether breeders have gone far enough to exploit the remunerative foreign and Commonwealth markets. My own belief is that there is a large market still to be found, for it is certain it has never been explored sufficiently except by a few, and then only by the bigger studs. If there is truth in what I say, where are these markets to be found?

The great importing country for many years past has been the United States of America, which must over the years have absorbed hundreds of English bred Arabs. That they have a great number of the breed in the country is well known, and that many of these are of the highest class is true. Nonetheless, and in spite of restrictions, there is still a demand for the best we can show them. Visitors from that country inspect the English studs fairly regularly and buyers come too from Holland where there are several studs, one or two of fair size. But the United States can be fairly looked upon as a market still open for the best stock.

So far as other parts of the Western Hemisphere are concerned there is a small market for Arabs in Brazil, for breeding stock-horses, and for the same purpose in Canada. Arabs are also bought for showing and for the unending joy of just riding for pleasure. Canada is certainly a market very much open. When we consider the vastness of the Western Hemisphere it should make the mouths of all breeders water!

The Dutch nation tends to be horse-minded and even in this mechanical age a traveller through Holland is as likely, in a journey of 20 minutes, to see as many horses grazing as he would in one hour in England, if indeed he would see any at all in some parts of the country. In the year following the end of the last war I judged a mere handful of Arabs for the Netherlands Arabian Horse Club at Arnhem. To-day one has only to look at their Stud Book to realize what a large number of registrations have been made. Exports are made to England and the U.S.A. from time to time, and I hear that some have gone to Germany and the Scandinavian countries. Dr Houtappel of the Rodania Stud, Laren, in Holland, has made some notable purchases from Poland. Other than the Polish-Arab, the Dutch Arabians are probably all based on pure

English stock and there is a small, but fairly regular, shipment from England to Holland each year.

One might well consider Germany as a possible export market, and the fact that its Western borders are no great distance away is worth noting. Germany is a country of outstandingly good types of horses, such as Holsteins, Hanoverians, Trakehners and Mecklenburgs. Although a nation with a strong leaning towards the heavier type of saddle horse, Arab blood has been much used in the past in various of their breeds. In a small way they are acquiring Arabs from time to time and I have met nationals from that country in Holland engaged in this very act. If the demand from Germany should increase, and I think this is more likely than not, some publicity to this end might encourage an export trade which would be to the advantage of the breeders here.

From Germany to Scandinavia. Sweden has in the last few years imported Arabs and I personally receive enquiries from time to time. It is surprising how the arrival in a country of one or two good Arabians, truly typical of their breed and, perhaps as much as anything, having an abundance of Arabian elegance and charm, seems to induce further importations. I know little of sales to those other Scandinavian countries, Norway and Denmark, but importations are made in small numbers. I have yet to hear of Arab horses being shipped to Iceland. That all three countries are no great distance away should be a helpful factor.

Has anyone heard of Arabs being exported to Belgium or to Switzerland? If there have been any it is doubtful whether there have been more than a very few. I have never heard of any interest in the breed being shown by either of those countries, but theoretically there is no reason why Arabs should not be bred and used there just as they are in Holland. The Belgians have always been known for producing good horses, though it must be admitted of the heavier types such as the Ardennes and Brabant or Belgian Heavy Draught horse. The Swiss rank prominently as equestrians and not so much as horse breeders, although there are notable stud farms in the country.

An outstanding French saddle horse is the Tarbenian, a breed which originated in Tarbes, a small town at the foot of the Pyrenees; a light boned horse of some 15 hands, the Tarbenian has a more than ordinarily good reputation. It is sufficient to say here that it is practically an Anglo-Arab, as for many many years now nothing but Arab and Thoroughbred blood has been used. That is by the way. What is of interest to breeders of Arabs in this country is to learn of a revived interest in the Arab breed by a small, but enthusiastic, group of Frenchmen, in which the veterinary profession is included. They have recently formed an Arab Horse Society which is called Groupement des Amateur du Cheval Arabe et des Derivés. This latter includes Barbs and Andalusians.

No reference to the Arab in France can be considered complete without reference to the Government Stud of Anglo-Arabs, Haras de Pompadour, long established in the ancient and truly romantic town bearing that name. On a recent visit there I learnt of the existence of two pure-bred stallions, and saw one of them which had been imported from North Africa. This was a new importation which, although time had not permitted the sight of any of his gets, was apparently exactly what the authorities there desired, especially as this line of breeding was entirely to their liking. Beyond saying that this young horse had fine limbs and was of an impressively hardy sort, it was almost entirely lacking in the type we look for in this country, and seemed devoid of any outstanding grace or charm. But handsome is as handsome does, and if this newcomer produces stock up to the standard of the Pompadour Anglo-Arabs and Part-bred Arabs, of which I saw many examples, then there can be no grumbles. Much could be written to delight the horse-lover of the charm of Pompadour which seems truly to live up to its romantic name. The paddocks filled with mares and foals remain a lovely memory.

I have not had the opportunity of studying the pedigrees which will no doubt be the basis of this new French Stud Book, but I anticipate these will consist mainly of North African blood. From correspondence and personal conversation with various

Queen of the Meadows. Part-bred Arab. Bay Mare (Count D'Orsaz/-Foxgrove).

Indriss. Chestnut Stallion (Indian Magic/Rissalma). (Photo by A. Brown and Co.)

Golden Sally. Part-bred Arab. Chestnut Mare (Jaleel/Roma). (Photo by Miles Bros.)

Khada. Bay Gelding (Rifaria/Kabara).

members it is clear some of the Arabs in France lack the essential characteristics of the English-bred horse, the absence of the pronounced dish in the face-line and the lack of breadth and general scope in the quarters being among them. As the English Arab of to-day (in the absence now of the horse in the desert) is the fountain head of the breed as it spreads throughout the world, it would seem logical for the new French Society to import a good nucleus from England.

As this is the position in France, English breeders, with the co-operation of these enthusiastic Frenchmen, who have, incidentally, already imported some of our stock, could well have a ready market right on their doorstep!

In reviewing the position of the pure-bred Arabian in France to-day it is an extraordinary fact, elicited from enquiries made during my visit there, that the number of either sex is almost negligible, and yet France is a country which for centuries has specialised in the direct product of Arab breeding. When one remembers the size of the country it is really remarkable, especially too if we recall the great numbers of the breed in so many other countries, notably U.S.A., Great Britain and elsewhere as I have shown.

The British have shown that nothing encourages the breeding of horses more than developing the child rider. One can only wish that France may follow the advice I gave to breeders in the Netherlands some years ago to buy New Forest ponies to supply suitable mounts for children, of which that country had but a negligible quantity. That was only some five or six years ago; to-day they have, I am told, some two thousand. The Arab will always, anywhere, make its mark on its own merits as a pure-bred and will prove of the greatest value for cross-breeding, as has been amply demonstrated throughout the ages.

Despite the restrictions I have mentioned, the Stud Book shows a considerable number of Arabs exported to Australia, where they are used for show and particularly for breeding stock horses for cattle raising. There is not, as yet, any great demand from New Zealand, but South Africa is certainly interested in breeding a range and pleasure horse, and also has Arab classes at the principal shows.

I have already referred to the vast lands of Brazil and Canada and if we add to these all the other countries I have mentioned, as well as bearing in mind many more which could be potential markets, we need have no fear of the door being shut on exporters for fear of overcrowding, rather one might expect a welcome for all immigrants!

If all that I have said gives the true position, then it may well be asked—how is the individual to enter this Breeders' Eldorado? Most export sales in the past have been made by sellers using their own methods of introduction and approach, and by receiving visitors from abroad who have been attracted by the success of certain stallions and mares at the Society's Annual Shows. We might well advertise officially to the effect, 'You want the best Arabs, we have them!'

In most of these potential export countries papers are published either solely devoted to the Arab breed, or to general equine or equestrian matters. I can't help feeling that advertisements in such papers, announcing our ability to supply high class Arabs and offering a list of the studs prepared to sell, is the sort of thing required, and I can imagine few better ways of spending some of the Society's funds. If, however, the Society felt unable to sponsor such a scheme, I think a few of the bigger breeders might well combine to launch something of this sort.

CHAPTER ELEVEN

The Anglo-Arab

The Anglo-Arab is the Thoroughbred/Arab cross which, in fact, is a union of great antiquity, as for centuries now horse-breeders have recognised the obvious worth which must result from such a mating. This composite breed is, therefore, well established throughout the world, with breeders seeming to prefer the use of the Arab on the Thoroughbred mare rather than vice-versa, although, of course, this is not always so and there is no official directive on the point. It might be thought that claiming parentage from two such world famous breeds the progeny would be the horse of near perfection, but while many beautiful examples have been known and will, no doubt, continue to be bred, no one of any knowledge of horse-breeding will be deceived by the thought that near perfection will necessarily be the result of such breeding.

However that may be, it is claimed that in the Anglo-Arab, born of sound stock and whose parents conform to a high standard, not only of conformation, but of the respective classic types of each breed, is to be found a horse of outstanding quality possessed of more intelligence than is found in the normal Thoroughbred and, with even more certainty, having sounder limbs and cleaner wind. It is for these reasons that the Anglo-Arab is claimed to be the ideal horse for use as hunter, hack, in steeplechases, three-day events, point-to-points, show jumping and dressage competitions. A formidable claim but one which can be substantiated.

Record must be made here of the only conditions under which

the Arab Horse Society will admit any horse to its Anglo-Arab Stud Book:

(1) Horses in whose pedigree there is no strain of blood other than Thoroughbred or Arab. To comply with this condition Thoroughbreds must be entered, or eligible for entry, in the General Stud Book, and Arabs must be entered, or eligible for entry, in the G.S.B. (Arab Section) or the Arab Horse Stud Book.

(2) Anglo-Arabs bred in foreign countries entered, or eligible for entry, in the recognised Stud Books of those countries may also be accepted for registration if approved by the Council.

It is a little strange in a world inhabited by well over 100 different breeds of horses and ponies, and a considerable number more if some little known breeds claiming specific local names were recognised, that England and France should be the only countries which unite the Thoroughbred and the Arab and give the progeny a name. Strictly speaking this should be confined to England and its Anglo-Arabs only, but, in fact, France has developed, and has for about a century and a half, the well-known and very excellent Tarbenian horse which I have mentioned. It must be pointed out, however, that this horse had its origin in a breed descended from Navarre blood, which in turn derived from the Andalusian horse. Briefly, following considerable deterioration over the years, English Thoroughbred blood was introduced. It was later found necessary to abandon this and to bring in Arab blood. Then by a process of continually associating the two breeds, the Arab and the Thoroughbred, over a period of some 150 years the elegant Tarbenian was evolved. It is recognised now as an Anglo-Arab.

France has too her famous and ancient Government controlled Haras de Pompadour, where Anglo-Arab and Part-bred Arabs have been bred for centuries and to which I referred in my chapter dealing with exports.

The Anglo-Arab has, of course, been bred, and continues to be bred in other countries, but so far as I know it has no Stud Books other than the English and French ones. Nonetheless, apart from

Indian Magic. Grey Stallion (Raktha/Indian Crown). (Photo by John Nestle)

Dargee. Chestnut Stallion (Manasseh/Myola).

Celina. Bay Mare (Witraz/Elza). Bred in Poland. (Photo by Photonews)

Domatella. Chestnut Mare (Blue Domino/Umatella).

Ringing Gold. Chestnut Stallion (Mikeno/-Gleaming Gold).

Nawarra. Chestnut Mare (Trypolis/Najada). (Photo by Photonews)

Hanif. Grey Stallion (Silver Vanity/Sirella).

Mikoletta. Chestnut Mare (Mikeno/Myoletta). (Photo by Photonews)

Marinella. Grey Mare (Indian Magic/Myolanda). (Photo by Photonews)

these countries the breed is very well favoured for various activities, particulary for show jumping and dressage, to both of which it is well suited and has been shown with success from time to time, in the hands mostly of foreign competitors, at the Royal International Horse Show and other big shows here and on the continent. Despite all this and in the absence of any adverse criticism of the breed, why is not the Anglo-Arab more popular in this country? That this is true I will endeavour to show by official figures of the number of entries into the Stud Book, and also entries at the Society's Annual Show:

Stud Book Registrations

	1965	1964	1963	1962	1961	1960	1959
ARABS	210	221	180	137	118	140	108
ANGLO-ARABS	49	50	40	35	49	55	53
PART-BREDS	692	679	508	452	333	400	347

Show Entries

	1966	1965	1964	1963	1962	1961	1960	1959
ARABS	252	247	207	203	173	130	120	133
ANGLO-ARABS	101	77	69	83	67	54	47	53
PART-BREDS	250	239	242	199	197	211	172	166

If we take the Stud Book Registrations, little more than a casual glance will show that whereas the Pure-breds and the Part-breds have shown a marked general overall increase in numbers during the eight years, the Anglo-Arabs do not show anything like so satisfactory a result.

Various explanations can be given to explain why the Anglo-Arab seems to have taken third place in popularity in the minds of breeders, and it may be that more by omission than commission they have allowed this to come about. The Pure-bred must, for various reasons, hold an advantage, for he is by far the more saleable animal and his price, on the average, much in excess of those of his two off-shoots, although in saleability we must not forget the potential of the good Part-bred Show Pony, which is very high. Could the Arab Horse Society and/or the Anglo-Arab breeders have done more for the breed?

Yes, I think they could, had the breed's capabilities in so many spheres of equestrian sport been fully, and more generally, recognised in the past. If the qualities of the Anglo-Arab are now appreciated there is every reason to believe their numbers will increase in the future.

The first of these qualities is the Anglo-Arab's suitability for dressage. Typical of the refined type of riding horse and of suitable size, with the required elegance which is surely an asset, it is fair to assume that it has just that extra bit of intelligence to give an advantage over the Thoroughbred. It is not necessarily exactly intelligence, although that may be true enough, it is the presumed ability and willingness to apply itself to the arduous and prolonged course of tuition required by dressage. It is an accepted fact that the Arab is favoured as the Liberty horse of the circus because, apart from his beauty and glamourous appearance, he is a model pupil, especially the stallion, which rarely turns sour in work. Isn't it fair to assume that the Anglo-Arab inherits something of this? Results would seem to point this way.

From dressage we are led naturally to 'Event' horses, a curious title to describe a horse which has or is likely to make its mark in Three-day Events. The title, it seems, has come to stay, and why not, for it seems apt enough? What does this involve? The first phase as we know is dressage, the second, steeplechase and cross country, to which the Anglo-Arab is admirably suited, as apart from his ability to jump, which is not in doubt, we can surely hope that he has inherited something of the Arab's renowned stamina and soundness. I would repeat stamina and soundness, for these are of transcending importance in Three-day Event competitions. Of the third phase—the Anglo-Arab's power to jump the regulation British Show Jumping Association's course—I suggest he is as fitted as any, and as to his ability to pull out sound on the third day for this phase, he should have few superiors.

The Society holds a class at its show for Anglo-Arabs under

saddle which, according to the 1964 catalogue, is open to stallions, mares and geldings, and, in this year it collected an entry of nine. I noticed a special reserve was given for those not exceeding 14·2 h.h. Do we, by the way, want to produce Anglo-Arabs as small as this, when our Part-bred seem to fit so well what is, after all, a pony class?

Another thought to encourage the breeding of the Anglo-Arab: cannot some support be given at the Society's and other Shows in the form of 'Specials' for the best light-weight hunter? No support is given anywhere, as far as I know, to Anglo-Arabs in jumping classes. A special for them and/or Part-bred Arabs would be very encouraging, and one might hope to see, one of these days, a class for show jumping confined to Arabs. Happily to-day the Arab and the Part-bred Arab show pony enjoy great popularity. Could not a big drive be made to help the Anglo-Arab to join them? Although this would entail a somewhat long term policy I think the breed has not only great potential, but has some advantages over both its relations.

CHAPTER TWELVE

The Part-bred Arab

Entry in the Arab Society's Part-bred Register is limited to those animals who have either one great-grandparent of pure Arab blood or two great-grandparents of pure Arab blood. This embraces a wide range, for it is possible thus to enter an Arab-Shetland cross, or to go to the other extreme, an Arab-Percheron! In fact, by far the greatest number of registrations consist of animals ranking in size as ponies—i.e. not exceeding 14·2 h.h.—and this no doubt for the reason that supply and demand, or rather the latter, dictates the quantum. There is probably little doubt that for the show ring to-day demand for ponies under 14·2 h.h. probably exceeds that of horses. That is a rough guess anyway.

Such being the case there is little wonder that the Part-bred Arab has a wide popularity for, apart from the Arab's influence in the pony world in general, and on the Show pony in particular, its possibilities in the larger animal ranging from 15 to 16 h.h. is very considerable. Visions of light-weight hunters, hacks, quality cobs, show-jumpers, polo ponies and Event-horses all loom among the likely ones, but there are not enough of these big Part-breds. Again I ask whether enough encouragement is given, and suggest that much of what I wrote on the subject of the Anglo-Arab is exactly applicable here.

By and large, whatever the breeder is aiming for, pure or cross-bred, he must always place quality very high in his scheme of things. Inevitably, therefore, unless for some reason he wishes to go outside the Arab or Thoroughbred, his choice must lie between the two. Their respective merits are too well-known to require further repetition here.

In the previous chapter I gave details of the number of Pure-bred Arabs entered in the Register and those entered at recent shows. To find nearly 700 admitted for entry in the Register, and over 200 entered at the Annual Show, in one year is impressive. It is interesting to note, and it seems natural enough, that for many years the number of Part-breds entered at the Society's Show have exceeded not only the Anglo-Arab but the Pure-breds as well, yet in 1963, for the first time, the Pure-bred went ahead. Is this to be the trend or was it just fortuitous? It was not repeated in the following year. I think for the good of the breed it hardly matters, for whichever the case, the numbers, if generally maintained, are so satisfactory that there can be no doubt whatever that the future is very wide open for the further, and greater, development of the Part-bred. Certainly the Society seems to encourage this, judging by the way they impartially allocate the classes at the Annual Show between the under and over 14·2 h.h.

It is at the Shows out in the country, however, where support and encouragement should be given in greater measure to this most useful Part-bred Arab, support which, if forthcoming, must emanate from the breeders and exhibitors either by promise of entries in classes specially for Anglo- or Part-breds, or special awards for these, preferably in breed classes. Saddle classes too can be very helpful, and when one remembers that either can provide the horse of size, substance and quality, the task is not a very formidable one.

I have in this chapter mentioned the polo pony, the Arab-bred polo pony, in which connection it is of some interest to look back into the past. Earlier volumes of the Arab Horse Stud Books show that at the National Pony Show, at the Royal International, Aldershot and elsewhere, Anglo-Arabs and Part-bred Arabs competed successfully in the heavy, middle and light-weight polo classes. The few of us who remember those days will recall the names of some of the Arab-bred entries, Dunducket and Nantucket, both heavy weights, Malanya and Malasmin, Malinky and others, names which now mean little to the present-day horsemen but were then of real importance. Those were the days when the polo-bred, as distinct from the Argentine and small Thoroughbred of the day, were highly prized.

Few trends in the horse world of this century have been more marked than the change in children's riding ponies, and here I refer in particular to the show-pony, which is almost invariably shown in three classes, not exceeding 12·2 h.h., 13·2 h.h. and 14·2 h.h. respectively. Custom, or the unwritten law of the show ring, decrees that the overriding and final criterion is quality, and it is curious, but, I think, an undoubted fact, that this is so *whatever* the breed may be. Good children's ponies were to be found in the old days—I speak now of the early years of the century—in show classes at Ranelagh and Hurlingham, at the International, in those days held at Olympia in London, and of course at 'The Hall' (the 'London Show') as the National Pony Society's Show at the Agricultural Hall was called.

How very far removed, however, were the ponies of those days from the delightful, but as many think over exquisite, dainty and altogether charming show pony of these days. Although many of the former were justly admired I admit that, were they stood up against to-day's best show ponies, most would appear as 'commoners'. Whether the change has been a move for the better, or whether it would have been wiser to have retained more of the characteristics of the less elegant and refined, is a matter on which horsemen differ, and anyway is hardly a subject for this chapter. That they were tougher, possessed of greater stamina and were less temperamental is probably true, and, therefore, they were perhaps more strictly the ideal mount for children.

Such then being the trend, the show pony breeder had two avenues of breeding to explore and he has done so very thoroughly. On the distaff side, there was the whole range of mares from the Mountain and Moorland group, while the obvious source for the sires was from Arabs and Thoroughbreds. In this sphere the latter has been most successful as countless examples have shown, and so is the very formidable rival to the Arab. For a number of years past the show-pony classes have been a battle ground for the off-spring of these two premier breeds, and the day might have gone against the Arab but for a line of exceptionally successful Arab bred ponies, which for some years swept all before them. I have already referred to the ponies sired by the grey Arab, Naseel, in particular to the mare Pretty Polly out of Gypsy Gold, which, possessed of great charm and elegance, won everywhere for a long period in the 13·2 h.h. classes. Although not so outstandingly successful as their sister, literally a host of other ponies, mostly in the same class, undoubtedly caused many breeders with show pony aspirations to seek similar fame from among the Arabs. This resulted in the production, by a variety of sires, of many more prize-winning Part-bred Arabs, a factor obviously beneficial to the stallion owner.

It is well-known that to-day Holland is the home of a large number of our New Forest ponies, both Forest and Dutch Forest-bred; in fact there are some 2,000 I am told. From a recent official publication, issued by the Arabian Horse Society of the Netherlands, it is clear that the Dutch are becoming most interested in the development of the Arab-Dutch New Forest riding pony, and no doubt this cross will be seen there in ever increasing numbers. The new found popularity of the Mountain and Moorland pony from Great Britain is a remarkable part in the story of our native ponies, and this vital link with the Horse of the Desert is something which must appeal to all who watch the development of the horse.

CHAPTER THIRTEEN

The Arab and its Uses

The question is sometimes asked of what real use is the Arab? Why isn't it employed in more ways, or is it just something rather beautiful, but of little practical value, which people like to have about the place—a sort of equine status symbol perhaps? Without wishing on behalf of the Arab to say to breeders of other horses—anything you can do we can do better, let us see what the Arab *can* do, what he has omitted to do, and in the latter case, how and why this could and should be rectified. For what purpose and why are horses normally kept? To ride, to drive, to show and, even in these days, to play a part in earning a living for many people. This latter is almost entirely the case with the racehorse.

The Arab is pre-eminently a saddle horse, and if we look back through the ages we find it was as such that the Bedouins of the Arabian Desert used him. To the Bedouins he was, with the camel, a means of transport in their ceaseless wanderings and an essential aid in hunting the gazelle with the Saluki hound. Furthermore, and of greater importance, he was a vital factor in their very existence in the endless desert tribal warfare. We are not, however, concerned with those times and happenings, excepting only to the extent that the Arab has for centuries been associated with the saddle.

I do not necessarily subscribe to the idea, which in these days seems to be held by so many, that if you have a horse or pony you must use it for sport, display, or some form of competition. I am not averse to this sort of thing, far from it, but I have always thought there is in the horse-world nothing to touch the extraordinary

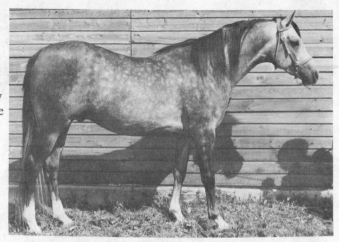

idi Bou Sbeyel. Grey
tallion (Mikeno/The
ady Ida).

Crystal Fire. Chestnut
Stallion (Dargee/-
Rosinella).

Amorella. Chestnut Mare
(General Grant/-
Domatella). (Photo by
Photonews)

Magic Flame. Bay Stallion (Indian Magic/Farissla).

Farjeca. Chestnut Mare (Grojec/Farette).

pleasure of riding just for the sake of riding, riding to enjoy the countryside, companionship with a friend if you like, but always the companionship of the horse. All this a man or woman, boy or girl can find on the back of an Arab; he's a good companion too, as good as you will find in the world of horses, and if you like some extra intelligence in your companion, there you are likely to find it!

And driving? Alas, where can we find the peaceful roads to travel? Is there any real future for the harness horse? Paradoxically in the last few years, born of enduring enthusiasm by the lover of the horse between the shafts, and I think, too, through most exceptionally good organisation, the British Driving Society has not only come into existence but really grows in strength in many parts of the country; in short it may be said to flourish within its very confined limits.

That the Arab is an excellent harness horse is well known, and for those who may doubt this, let me mention that many photographs and other forms of illustrations exist to prove the point. The present day hackney may, or rather most certainly does, excel in brilliant and dynamic action, and is a most delightful sight to see, yet in charm, grace and abounding elegance it has its equal in the Arab. The pity of it is that we hardly know where to find the Arab in harness to-day. What a chance awaits some Arab owners to 'hang one in harness', as the old-time dealer would say when he suggested putting a horse between the shafts. If most roads give but a chilly welcome to the harness horse, the British Driving Society, and many shows, give plenty of opportunities to drivers to display their turn-outs, and what charm there lies in that.

To ride and to drive? That the Arab is well qualified to fill the bill here is certain. With these two activities I mention breeding. When people ask of what use is the Arab, could they think that breeding is of so little importance that it can be brushed aside as of little moment? Do they forget (or perhaps they do not know) that in all the recognised breeds and types of horses and ponies to be found throughout the world, and of which I have said there are well over 100, the Arab has in numbers *played a greater part in them than any other breed, not excepting that wonder of the horse-world, the English Thoroughbred.* Why? Because the Arab combines the greatest number of equine virtues, and by reason of another unique fact, his prepotency is so very high—the highest, in fact, in the horse world. If all this be true, then I think one might fairly ask why worry about the many things an Arab should do? However that may be, let us consider some other activities.

Of perhaps little practical help, but obviously of considerable publicity value, is the use of the Arab as a display horse. In these days it is becoming ever harder to compete with the desperate competition in the entertainment world. This is particularly so when one remembers that horse shows contain a number of show classes, such as hacks, hunters, cobs, hackneys and ponies, none of which have over-much *general public* appeal. Why not use the Arab more in costume classes, or rather, why not confine some costume classes solely to Arabs as they do in the U.S.A. Although I can only judge from photographs, I understand, and can believe, that these parades are very attractive when authentic Western costume and tack are used, and I should imagine a class in Bedouin costume would be equally so.

I wonder what sort of support would be received, initially, from the members of the Society, for that presumably is where it would have to start. Such a display would add a great deal of charm and colour to our show rings. Two horse shows come to my mind as predominately receptive to new ideas—Richmond and Windsor. I feel if the Arab Horse Society, or a group of its members, could organise one or other of the suggested displays, exactly correct in all details, and having a sufficient number of entries, it could be a tremendous success.

While still on the subject of the Arab as what we might call a stage performer, I might mention that my stallion, Jaleel, appeared in a somewhat spectacular part in Korda's film production of *The Thief of Baghdad*, and would have done so again in his *Four*

Feathers (I think this was the film) had not a good friend, and a brother actor of Jaleel's, a cheetah, when they were close to each other during an interval at rehearsals, sprung at a sparrow, which sent Jaleel up and over backwards. Small damage was suffered, but an understudy had to be brought in. From among the many other horses engaged, Korda gave the lead to my Arab, not only for his presence, but because of his ability to face up to crowds, vividly moving colour, noise, gunfire and fire, to none of which did he show any concern; his 'chocolate horse' Korda called him, for Jaleel was a liver chestnut.

As further instances of the Arab as an actor, in the three Pageants in which I have appeared, I rode Arabs in two of them. At the Battle Abbey pageant I rode Jaleel, who by the way was bred by Lady Wentworth at Crabbet Park, and at Runnymede pageant, a chestnut mare, Capella, bred by the Prince of Wales. Both of these took leading equestrian parts which were of a somewhat spectacular kind, and neither was at all concerned with bands, crowds, or other disturbances. With this, I think we can say the Arab is a stage and film star in his own right, and can be relied on to exhibit charm, grace and romance, and where required, a bold front and outstanding courage!

It is not surprising that the Arab is not used in greater numbers as a hunter, when we consider that the normal man or woman who follows hounds prefer their hunters to be of a greater height than is to be found in the Arab, which does not exceed say 15·1 h.h. at the outside, and this is higher than the great majority of breeders, particularly the purists, rightly prefer. No doubt the views of these hunting people are sound enough, for a fence of any size on a small horse may appear a most formidable affair as it rushes towards them, while on a sixteen-hander such an obstacle may look like just one cavalletti on top of another!

The question of weight, however, is another matter altogether, for it is an undisputed fact that it is very hard to get to the bottom of the weight-carrying powers of the breed. In this connection I might mention that in 1920, when the first of the Endurance

Tests was held by the Arab Horse Society, the Committee, of which I was a member, when formulating the conditions for the 60 miles per day for five consecutive days, and ultimately deciding on 13 stone to be the weight carried, seriously considered, as more nearly approximating to the weight carried by the troop horse of those days, weights varying up to 17 stone! The Committee were all practical horsemen with cavalry officers among them who knew the Army requirements and the Arab in the East.

As to jumping ability, I would say the Arab is a fearless jumper, if a little unorthodox, and I hope I am not painting too pretty a picture when I say that, temperamentally, he'll probably have a bash at anything and therefore any light-weight is likely to be well served on an Arab. There are not many Arabs to be found with hounds, although probably the number will increase with the ever growing numbers which are being bred. Of well-known stallions being hunted at the present time I can think of Mary Sellar's Blue Halo, Patricia Lindsay's Rushti, Lady Hugh Russell's Touch of Magic, and Margaret Evans's Kami, Listopad and Naplyv.

That the Arab is well suited to polo its past history has shown, but to-day he could not live with the pace at which the game is played. Polo must, therefore, be ruled out as an activity for the breed, and so far as one can see, there is little likelihood of its return to the game, at any rate for top-class polo.

Spasmodically, during the century, races confined to Arabs have been tried in this country, but I should say with little success. It is a sport which appeals to few Arab breeders here, and to see Arabs raced makes no appeal to the public, who are almost wholly interested in racing as a medium for betting. It would be a long time, and many Arabs would have to be engaged, before they individually acquired racing form. Anyway, they could not race against the Thoroughbred (the speed of the latter, of course, would put paid to that) although many Arabs are registered in the Special Section of the General Stud Book. Weatherby and Sons, who publish the Stud Book, announced, in the latter part of 1965, that the section devoted to Arabs would not be included in future editions. Arabs have featured in the Stud Book since the appearance of the first volume in 1791.

Nonetheless, this question of racing is interesting from another point of view. The Arab in Poland is bred at Government Studs, and it is certain that it is carried out with the greatest care and directed and supervised by experts, for Poland has always been noted as a great horse-breeding country. Part of their scheme of breeding is that all horses intended for breeding must be raced, and only those who stand up to this test by remaining sound are bred from. I attribute much of the undoubted worth of the Polish-Arab, particularly its sound limbs, to this policy. To emphasize the importance given to racing where breeding is concerned, the same conditions are in force at the French Government Stud at Pompadour so far as their imported stallions are concerned. For this reason I believe it would be good for the breed in England could the racing test be applied here or anywhere else so far as that goes, but this is of course impossible. Think too of the increased cachet publicity of this kind would give to our stallions which are exported to the U.S.A. and Canada, to Australia and South Africa and elsewhere, for breeding stock horses. The alternative to racing is, of course, to race the horses against the clock. If less interesting the end product could be of equal value.

This brings one logically to the question of endurance, at which the Arab excels. The whole history of endurance of the horse in all parts of the world is packed with endless examples, all of which are very confusing when it comes to comparisons, for varying distances and weights have to be read in conjunction with speeds, and a 24 hour test with perhaps one of 24 days. There may too be the question of Arabs only, or Arabs against the world. One thing seems fairly certain, and it is that history points to the Arab being, in this particular sphere, the superior to all others. But as I have said, great confusion of mind is likely to those who study the records. In the light of the obvious use of Anglo-Arabs and Part-bred Arabs in Three-day Event trials and hunting, I think the question of endurance is now acquiring a greater significance than it has for many years past, and I must, in consequence, touch on a little early history of the Society.

It will be realised that the years of the Society's Endurance Tests in 1920/21/22 were those immediately following the end of the First World War, during which enormous numbers of horses were used by the combatants, this country being no exception. While it was recognised that during the war mechanical transport had been introduced and was being developed, nonetheless it was assumed that should hostilities ever break out again (we only had to wait 20 years!) horses would have to be used once more. The Arab breed having always been in favour for cross-breeding horses for war purposes, more so by other countries by the way, the Council thought it well to re-establish and bring to the notice of those who might be concerned, the endurance of the Arab.

The tests were held, and it is as well to recall that when the distance and weights were considered (300 miles divided into 60 miles a day for five consecutive days—weight 13 stone—as I have mentioned before) a silver challenge cup was added for the best time. Any condition such as this, in a way, removed strictly the question of endurance from the contest, and turned the whole affair more into a long distance race, which to my mind was not only unnecessary but unfair to the horse.

However that may be, in the 1922 test I rode the bay stallion Swaiman not for the 'race', but for the gold medal, which he won. I mention the following not only as a tribute to a very splendid horse, but to show how even ridden at a fast pace, pushing on relentlessly all day, day after day, this stallion could have gone on, for how long no one could say. He had in fact, although beaten for time over the five days, finished first (some 20 minutes I believe) in front of the next horse in. Having been on his back for 300 miles, and in spite of pressing on a bit harder during the last day, I am convinced, beyond any doubt whatever, that Swaiman could have continued at the same pace for an even greater length of time. All I can say, as an experienced horseman, and having been so closely associated with him for those five days, is that he *showed not the slightest indication of any distress.* He remained alert, interested and had a splendid appetite, he slept well and was a perfectly fit horse, having lost no condition so far as could be seen, a fact which was remarked on by many. These tests were watched by many knowledgeable horsemen, particularly by several of the Lewes racehorse trainers. On the morning of the sixth day when the test was over, and when the horses had to be passed for soundness, Swaiman's legs were clean and cool and he showed not the slightest sign of wear. *And he carried five stone of dead weight.*

From whatever angle we look at it, this was a very remarkable example of great endurance, with the horse ending up in as good a condition as when he started. That was real endurance, and I have no reason to suppose, good horse though Swaiman was, that the average Arab is not capable of similarly excelling in stamina and endurance. With such in mind, it seems to me to be something which might well be considered in the breeding of Event horses and the lighter-weighted hunters.

With the concluding commentary on the powers of endurance found in the Arab I would like to add a true and moving story of the breed's extreme courage and endurance and its amazing powers of recuperation. It relates to a 14·3 h.h., 13 year-old bay mare belonging to the Chief of the Muteyr tribe. During a battle between the Shammar Bedouins and the Mutain Afman, the Chief was killed, whereupon his slave rode the mare 180 miles in three days. It is interesting to note this 60 miles a day average is the distance covered by the English Endurance Tests, although they were for 300 miles at an average of 60 miles a day. There in a sense the similarity ends, except in regard to total distance, for the desert ride was in the appalling temperature of 170° *F. and the mare had not a drink of water.* She was brought into Kuwait a week after the battle.

The above was authenticated by the late Colonel H. R. P. Dixon who wrote: 'I had her secretly stabled in a house near my own where I fed and tended her for three months with the help of my wife. We gave her nothing but lucerne, dates in the form of a mash and milk to drink for the first fortnight of her stay'. Colonel Dixon added that she was a beautiful mare with large round eyes, and a broad forehead and with a very small mouth and nostrils. It would be interesting to know to what age this mare lived and whether she had any foals, and if so, how many, after this terrific and surely unique test of endurance. Anyway the story seems to have had a happy ending.

If it is true to say that the Society has been slow in showing the Arab as anything more than a show-horse, and this is not altogether accurate, there were signs in the year 1965 of commendable efforts to put this right. In the lovely country surrounding Goodwood in Sussex and at Fakenham in Norfolk, two- and one-day events open to Arabs, Anglo-Arabs and Part-bred Arabs were held on modest lines, those responsible wisely considering that it was better to feel the way with caution, and thus test response and results. Both events were successful and evidently greatly enjoyed.

It is probable that these early efforts will be continued and possibly increased in number. If they are, every effort must be made to run them on more ambitious lines (though still with a cautious approach), remembering that all over the country to-day similar events, so far as dressage, show jumping and cross-country riding are concerned, are held by almost innumerable Riding Clubs and Pony Club branches. It is true that long distance rides form no part of the general run of the latter, but if Goodwood and Fakenham or any other project include distance rides (and I think this is essential) something more severe than a day's ride of 50 miles under 11 stone 7 lbs is surely expected of an Arab.

In the same year an open 50 mile ride was held in the neighbourhood of Exmoor. Sponsored by a leading London daily paper, it received very wide publicity and was very successful. There is no doubt the impression was given to the public at large, naturally ignorant of the capabilities of the horse, that those who completed the ride of 50 miles in the day had accomplished something to wonder at. How many hunters in the course of a season, in the appalling 'going' of a typical English day's hunting, including probably dozens of fences to be negotiated, travel approximately this distance or even more, especially with, say, the Devon and Somerset Staghounds? Certainly they did often in the old days before the motor horse box came into use. As to the Arab, it should not only be used in the various ways indicated in this chapter, but must be seen to be used, and in a way worthy of its capabilities.

For what then *can* the Arab be used? For any and every purpose for which other horses can be used, but primarily, as it always has been, for improving other breeds. For hunting, dressage, three-day events, polo, other than first-class, endurance tests, harness, many forms of display and parades and as a top class sire of show ponies, and we must not forget the Liberty horse of the circus. Apart from these it is fair to claim for the breed, beauty and charm beyond all others, but these have no bearing on performance. To those who ask of what use *is* the Arab, I think this Chapter gives a fair answer.

CHAPTER FOURTEEN

What Lies Ahead?

The future of the Arab must be, to a large extent, that of all saddle horses, for surely no one can be so outrageously optimistic as to suggest that the harness horse will ever return to the days either of his usefulness, or those times when he added to the charm of the lovely gigs and curricles, the high-flyer phaetons and others of that elegant family. The age-old question asked by all thoughtful horsemen of how long the popularity of the horse will remain is still unanswered, unless it be that it will last at least the lifetime of even to-day's youngest riders' grandchildren!

Quite apart from the pleasure of all forms of competitive activities in which the saddle horse of to-day is engaged, I have always felt, and certainly nothing has happened to alter my views, that the association of horse and man is unique, and normally utterly full of pleasure. There is no other association between man and beast which approaches the joy of riding, riding the countryside; just that. There are still large areas, even in these days of car-packed roads, over which the horseman can ride and be happy, so let us take hope for all breeds and types of saddle horses and ponies, and particularly for the Arab.

By selective breeding it does not require over-much skill to alter vastly the type and/or size of any breed, and in the process eliminate certain features which have hitherto been considered essential, or, indeed, to introduce some that are perhaps almost completely alien. This has been proved in dog-breeding and there is no need to elaborate this fact by quoting examples.

To suggest that breeding on these lines is likely to occur in the

98

future in any specific breed of horses or ponies is very unlikely, but I am convinced that some danger lies ahead for the Arab. Can anyone question the fact that there are many Arabs to-day which lack the qualities of the true, well-known, well-defined and unmistakable Horse of the Desert in size, type and presence? That this is so surely cannot be denied, implying as it does that some wise selective breeding has been wanting. I have it from authority in the U.S.A. that similar danger lies in that country and causes concern. In short, too many Arabs are too off-type and of too great a height.

So long as the saddle horse survives so will the Arab. Let all who have it in their power see that the Arab of the future is the unmistakable Arab in all respects, utterly true to type, of great presence and very beautiful.

Index

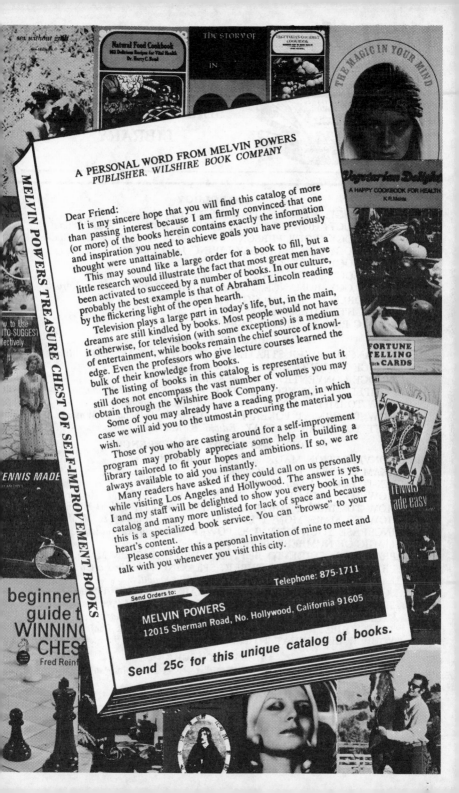

Melvin Powers
SELF-IMPROVEMENT
LIBRARY

ASTROLOGY

____ASTROLOGY: A FASCINATING HISTORY P. Naylor 2.00
____ASTROLOGY: HOW TO CHART YOUR HOROSCOPE Max Heindel 2.00
____ASTROLOGY: YOUR PERSONAL SUN-SIGN GUIDE Beatrice Ryder 2.00
____ASTROLOGY FOR EVERYDAY LIVING Janet Harris 2.00
____ASTROLOGY MADE EASY Astarte 2.00
____ASTROLOGY MADE PRACTICAL Alexandra Kayhle 2.00
____ASTROLOGY, ROMANCE, YOU AND THE STARS Anthony Norvell 3.00
____MY WORLD OF ASTROLOGY Sydney Omarr 3.00
____THOUGHT DIAL Sydney Omarr 2.00
____ZODIAC REVEALED Rupert Gleadow 2.00

BRIDGE & POKER

____ADVANCED POKER STRATEGY & WINNING PLAY A. D. Livingston 2.00
____BRIDGE BIDDING MADE EASY Edwin Kantar 5.00
____BRIDGE CONVENTIONS Edwin Kantar 4.00
____COMPLETE DEFENSIVE BRIDGE PLAY Edwin B. Kantar 10.00
____HOW TO IMPROVE YOUR BRIDGE Alfred Sheinwold 2.00
____HOW TO WIN AT POKER Terence Reese & Anthony T. Watkins 2.00
____TEST YOUR BRIDGE PLAY Edwin B. Kantar 3.00

BUSINESS STUDY & REFERENCE

____CONVERSATION MADE EASY Elliot Russell 2.00
____EXAM SECRET Dennis B. Jackson 2.00
____FIX-IT BOOK Arthur Symons 2.00
____HOW TO DEVELOP A BETTER SPEAKING VOICE M. Hellier 2.00
____HOW TO MAKE A FORTUNE IN REAL ESTATE Albert Winnikoff 3.00
____HOW TO MAKE MONEY IN REAL ESTATE Stanley L. McMichael 2.00
____INCREASE YOUR LEARNING POWER Geoffrey A. Dudley 2.00
____MAGIC OF NUMBERS Robert Tocquet 2.00
____PRACTICAL GUIDE TO BETTER CONCENTRATION Melvin Powers 2.00
____PRACTICAL GUIDE TO PUBLIC SPEAKING Maurice Forley 2.00
____7 DAYS TO FASTER READING William S. Schaill 2.00
____SONGWRITERS' RHYMING DICTIONARY Jane Shaw Whitfield 3.00
____SPELLING MADE EASY Lester D. Basch & Dr. Milton Finkelstein 2.00
____STUDENT'S GUIDE TO BETTER GRADES J. A. Rickard 2.00
____TEST YOURSELF — Find Your Hidden Talent Jack Shafer 2.00
____YOUR WILL & WHAT TO DO ABOUT IT Attorney Samuel G. Kling 2.00

CHESS & CHECKERS

____BEGINNER'S GUIDE TO WINNING CHESS Fred Reinfeld 2.00
____BETTER CHESS — How to Play Fred Reinfeld 2.00
____CHECKERS MADE EASY Tom Wiswell 2.00
____CHESS IN TEN EASY LESSONS Larry Evans 2.00
____CHESS MADE EASY Milton L. Hanauer 2.00
____CHESS MASTERY — A New Approach Fred Reinfeld 2.0
____CHESS PROBLEMS FOR BEGINNERS edited by Fred Reinfeld 2.0
____CHESS SECRETS REVEALED Fred Reinfeld 2.0
____CHESS STRATEGY — An Expert's Guide Fred Reinfeld 2.0

Melvin Powers
SELF-IMPROVEMENT
LIBRARY

_____CHESS TACTICS FOR BEGINNERS *edited by Fred Reinfeld*	2.00
_____CHESS THEORY & PRACTICE *Morry & Mitchell*	2.00
_____HOW TO WIN AT CHECKERS *Fred Reinfeld*	2.00
_____1001 BRILLIANT WAYS TO CHECKMATE *Fred Reinfeld*	2.00
_____1001 WINNING CHESS SACRIFICES & COMBINATIONS *Fred Reinfeld*	2.00

COOKERY & HERBS

_____CULPEPER'S HERBAL REMEDIES *Dr. Nicholas Culpeper*	2.00
_____FAST GOURMET COOKBOOK *Poppy Cannon*	2.50
_____HEALING POWER OF HERBS *May Bethel*	2.00
_____HERB HANDBOOK *Dawn MacLeod*	2.00
_____HERBS FOR COOKING AND HEALING *Dr. Donald Law*	2.00
_____HERBS FOR HEALTH How to Grow & Use Them *Louise Evans Doole*	2.00
_____HOME GARDEN COOKBOOK Delicious Natural Food Recipes *Ken Kraft*	3.00
_____NATURAL FOOD COOKBOOK *Dr. Harry C. Bond*	2.00
_____NATURE'S MEDICINES *Richard Lucas*	2.00
_____VEGETABLE GARDENING FOR BEGINNERS *Hugh Wiberg*	2.00
_____VEGETABLES FOR TODAY'S GARDENS *R. Milton Carleton*	2.00
_____VEGETARIAN COOKERY *Janet Walker*	2.00
_____VEGETARIAN COOKING MADE EASY & DELECTABLE *Veronica Vezza*	2.00
_____VEGETARIAN DELIGHTS — A Happy Cookbook for Health *K. R. Mehta*	2.00
_____VEGETARIAN GOURMET COOKBOOK *Joyce McKinnel*	2.00

HEALTH

_____DR. LINDNER'S SPECIAL WEIGHT CONTROL METHOD	1.00
_____GAYELORD HAUSER'S NEW GUIDE TO INTELLIGENT REDUCING	3.00
_____HELP YOURSELF TO BETTER SIGHT *Margaret Darst Corbett*	2.00
_____HOW TO IMPROVE YOUR VISION *Dr. Robert A. Kraskin*	2.00
_____HOW YOU CAN STOP SMOKING PERMANENTLY *Ernest Caldwell*	2.00
_____LSD — THE AGE OF MIND *Bernard Roseman*	2.00
_____MIND OVER PLATTER *Peter G. Lindner, M.D.*	2.00
_____NEW CARBOHYDRATE DIET COUNTER *Patti Lopez-Pereira*	1.00
_____PSYCHEDELIC ECSTASY *William Marshall & Gilbert W. Taylor*	2.00
_____YOU CAN LEARN TO RELAX *Dr. Samuel Gutwirth*	2.00

HOBBIES

_____BLACKSTONE'S MODERN CARD TRICKS *Harry Blackstone*	2.00
_____BLACKSTONE'S SECRETS OF MAGIC *Harry Blackstone*	2.00
_____COIN COLLECTING FOR BEGINNERS *Burton Hobson & Fred Reinfeld*	2.00
_____400 FASCINATING MAGIC TRICKS YOU CAN DO *Howard Thurston*	3.00
_____GOULD'S GOLD & SILVER GUIDE TO COINS *Maurice Gould*	2.00
_____HOW I TURN JUNK INTO FUN AND PROFIT *Sari*	3.00
_____HOW TO WRITE A HIT SONG & SELL IT *Tommy Boyce*	7.00
_____JUGGLING MADE EASY *Rudolf Dittrich*	2.00
_____MAGIC MADE EASY *Byron Wels*	2.00
_____SEW SIMPLY, SEW RIGHT *Mini Rhea & F. Leighton*	2.00
_____STAMP COLLECTING FOR BEGINNERS *Burton Hobson*	2.00
_____STAMP COLLECTING FOR FUN & PROFIT *Frank Cetin*	2.00

Melvin Powers
SELF-IMPROVEMENT
LIBRARY

MARRIAGE, SEX & PARENTHOOD

_____ABILITY TO LOVE *Dr. Allan Fromme* 3.00
_____ENCYCLOPEDIA OF MODERN SEX & LOVE TECHNIQUES *Macandrew* 2.00
_____GUIDE TO SUCCESSFUL MARRIAGE *Drs. Albert Ellis & Robert Harper* 3.00
_____HOW TO RAISE AN EMOTIONALLY HEALTHY, HAPPY CHILD, *A. Ellis* 2.00
_____IMPOTENCE & FRIGIDITY *Edwin W. Hirsch, M.D.* 2.00
_____NEW APPROACHES TO SEX IN MARRIAGE *John E. Eichenlaub, M.D.* 2.00
_____PSYCHOSOMATIC GYNECOLOGY *William S. Kroger, M.D.* 10.00
_____SEX WITHOUT GUILT *Albert Ellis, Ph.D.* 2.00
_____SEXUALLY ADEQUATE FEMALE *Frank S. Caprio, M.D.* 2.00
_____SEXUALLY ADEQUATE MALE *Frank S. Caprio, M.D.* 2.00
_____YOUR FIRST YEAR OF MARRIAGE *Dr. Tom McGinnis* 2.00

METAPHYSICS & OCCULT

_____BOOK OF TALISMANS, AMULETS & ZODIACAL GEMS *William Pavitt* 3.00
_____CONCENTRATION--A Guide to Mental Mastery *Mouni Sadhu* 2.00
_____DREAMS & OMENS REVEALED *Fred Gettings* 2.00
_____EXTRASENSORY PERCEPTION *Simeon Edmunds* 2.00
_____FORTUNE TELLING WITH CARDS *P. Foli* 2.00
_____HANDWRITING ANALYSIS MADE EASY *John Marley* 2.00
_____HANDWRITING TELLS *Nadya Olyanova* 3.00
_____HOW TO UNDERSTAND YOUR DREAMS *Geoffrey A. Dudley* 2.00
_____ILLUSTRATED YOGA *William Zorn* 2.00
_____IN DAYS OF GREAT PEACE *Mouni Sadhu* 2.00
_____KING SOLOMON'S TEMPLE IN THE MASONIC TRADITION *Alex Horne* 5.00
_____MAGICIAN — His training and work *W. E. Butler* 2.00
_____MEDITATION *Mouni Sadhu* 3.00
_____MODERN NUMEROLOGY *Morris C. Goodman* 2.00
_____NUMEROLOGY—ITS FACTS AND SECRETS *Ariel Yvon Taylor* 2.00
_____PALMISTRY MADE EASY *Fred Gettings* 2.00
_____PALMISTRY MADE PRACTICAL *Elizabeth Daniels Squire* 2.00
_____PALMISTRY SECRETS REVEALED *Henry Frith* 2.00
_____PRACTICAL YOGA *Ernest Wood* 2.00
_____PROPHECY IN OUR TIME *Martin Ebon* 2.50
_____PSYCHOLOGY OF HANDWRITING *Nadya Olyanova* 2.00
_____SEEING INTO THE FUTURE *Harvey Day* 2.00
_____SUPERSTITION — Are you superstitious? *Eric Maple* 2.00
_____TAROT *Mouni Sadhu* 4.00
_____TAROT OF THE BOHEMIANS *Papus* 3.00
_____TEST YOUR ESP *Martin Ebon* 2.00
_____WAYS TO SELF-REALIZATION *Mouni Sadhu* 2.00
_____WITCHCRAFT, MAGIC & OCCULTISM—A Fascinating History *W. B. Crow* 3.00
_____WITCHCRAFT — THE SIXTH SENSE *Justine Glass* 2.00
_____WORLD OF PSYCHIC RESEARCH *Hereward Carrington* 2.00
_____YOU CAN ANALYZE HANDWRITING *Robert Holder* 2.00

SELF-HELP & INSPIRATIONAL

_____ACT YOUR WAY TO SUCCESSFUL LIVING *Neil & Margaret Rau* 2.00
_____CYBERNETICS WITHIN US *Y. Saparina* 3.00
_____DAILY POWER FOR JOYFUL LIVING *Dr. Donald Curtis* 2.00
_____DOCTOR PSYCHO-CYBERNETICS *Maxwell Maltz, M.D.* 3.00
_____DYNAMIC THINKING *Melvin Powers* 1.00
_____GREATEST POWER IN THE UNIVERSE *U. S. Andersen* 4.00
_____GROW RICH WHILE YOU SLEEP *Ben Sweetland* 2.00
_____GROWTH THROUGH REASON *Albert Ellis, Ph.D.* 3.00
_____GUIDE TO DEVELOPING YOUR POTENTIAL *Herbert A. Otto, Ph.D.* 3.00
_____GUIDE TO HAPPINESS *Dr. Maxwell S. Cagan* 2.00
_____GUIDE TO LIVING IN BALANCE *Frank S. Caprio, M.D.* 2.00
_____GUIDE TO RATIONAL LIVING *Albert Ellis, Ph.D. & R. Harper, Ph.D.* 2.00
_____HELPING YOURSELF WITH APPLIED PSYCHOLOGY *R. Henderson* 2.00
_____HELPING YOURSELF WITH PSYCHIATRY *Frank S. Caprio, M.D.* 2.00
_____HOW TO ATTRACT GOOD LUCK *A. H. Z. Carr* 2.00

NOTES

NOTES